How to Be a Color Wizard

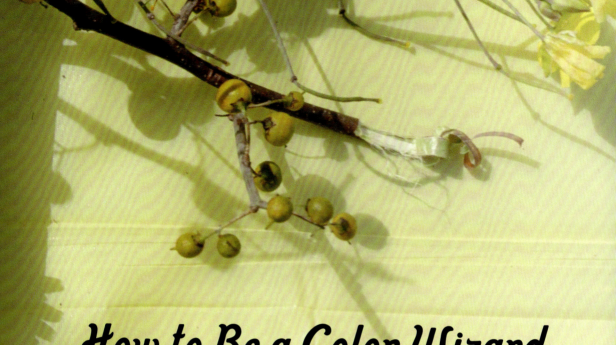

How to Be a Color Wizard

Forage and Experiment with Natural Art Making

Jason Logan

with photographs by Jason Fulford

mit Kids Press

Text copyright © 2024 by Jason Logan
Cover photographs: copyright © 2024 by Jason Logan and
Chloë Ellingson (front); copyright © 2024 by Jason Fulford (back)
Interior photographs copyright © 2024 by Jason Fulford and Chloë Ellingson
Blots (p. 101) from Mary Gartside, *An Essay on a New Theory of Colours,
and on Composition in General* (London: J. Barfield, 1808)
Additional images, hand-lettering, and illustrations by Jason Logan

All rights reserved. No part of this book may be reproduced, transmitted, or stored in an information retrieval system in any form or by any means, graphic, electronic, or mechanical, including photocopying, taping, and recording, without prior written permission from the publisher.

The MIT Press, the ☰mit Kids Press colophon, and MIT Kids Press are trademarks of The MIT Press, a department of the Massachusetts Institute of Technology, and used under license from The MIT Press. The colophon and MIT Kids Press are registered in the US Patent and Trademark Office.

First paperback edition 2025

Library of Congress Control Number: 2024930648
ISBN 978-1-5362-2940-0 (hardcover)
ISBN 978-1-5362-3975-1 (paperback)

25 26 27 28 29 30 CCP 10 9 8 7 6 5 4 3 2 1

Printed in Shenzhen, Guangdong, China

This book was typeset in Archer.

MIT Kids Press
an imprint of Candlewick Press
99 Dover Street
Somerville, Massachusetts 02144

mitkidspress.com
candlewick.com

EU Authorized Representative: HackettFlynn Ltd., 36 Cloch Choirneal, Balrothery,
Co. Dublin, K32 C942, Ireland. EU@walkerpublishinggroup.com

THIS BOOK IS FOR...

✱ Any kid who was told that it's just IMPOSSIBLE and did it anyway.

✱ Any adult who's learned how to say "Let's try it!"

✱ My family, who did a bit of BOTH.

CONTENTS

A Note to Wizard Assistants 4
What Kind of Wizard Are You Today? 7
    Now Find Your Wizard Element! 8
A Special Note to Young Wizards 10
Decoding the Secret Activity Symbols 11
The Seven Laws of Safe Sorcery 12

Part 1:
Gather!

Tool Up for Outdoor Adventure 16
    Assemble an Adventure-Worthy Color Wizard's Satchel 18
    Take Note: A Wizard's Notebook 21
    Make Your Own Wizard's Notebook 22
    How to Look Good: The Shrimp and the Hula-Hoop 26
    Make a Wizard's Paintbrush Wand 30
The Color Quests: Hunt for Hidden Color 34
    Quest 1. Wild Waters 38
    Quest 2. Enchanted Earth 40
    Quest 3. Color Falling from the Sky 42
    Quest 4. The Supernatural World 44

Part 2:
Transform!

How to (Temporarily) Turn Your Kitchen into a
  Secret Laboratory for Mad Wizardly Experiments 48

See-Through Sorcery: Five Cool Things Made from Glass
  That Are Great for Color Experiments 52

The Color Wizard's Secret Guide to Making Color from
  Practically Anything 54

The Rainbow Recipes 60
  Find a Rainbow in the Dark 62
  Take the Rainbow for a Walk 64
  RED: Bubbly, Fiery Dragon's Blood Ink 73
  MAGENTA: Bright-Pink (Underground) Ink 78
  ORANGE: Make a Martian Landscape 83
  ORANGEY-YELLOW: Spicy Highlighter Markers 87
  GREEN: Green Glow-in-the-Dark Plant Energy 91
  BLUE: Copper Penny Blue Ink 95
  INDIGO: Indigo Berry Blast Blobs 98
  PURPLE: The Enchanting Purple Lava Lamp 102

Beyond the Rainbow 106
  BROWN: Chocolate Jackson Pollock 108
  BLACK: How to Make Vine Charcoal for Ink or Drawing 110
    Dark Wizard Ink 112
    The Secret Life of the Color Black 114
  SILVER: Silvery Acorn Cap Ink 116
  GOLD: Golden-Green Ink 121
  CLEAR: Invisible Ink 124

Part 3:
Share!

- The Sorcerer's Shelf of Color Curiosities 130
- A Gathering of Wizards 133
  - The Acorn Store 134
  - Make Your Own Sidewalk Chalk 137
  - Say It with Potatoes 140
  - Natural Spray Paint 142
- Put the Party Together 145
  - A Color Block Party 146
  - The Psychedelic Sorcerer's Disco Party 148
  - A Rainbow Wizard Birthday 150
    - Natural Confetti 151
    - All-Natural Confetti Cannon 152
- The Last and Final Words of Advice for Wizards Who Have Made It to the End of This Book 154

- A Small Gallery of Works from Wizards in Training 156
- Acknowledgments 160
- Index 162

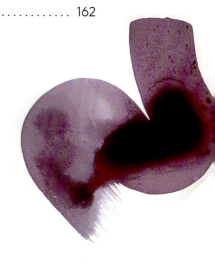

RIGHT NOW,

in your kitchen and just outside your front door,

are all the supplies you'll need

to start your quest to become

a full color wizard.

In this book you will find

secret recipes, magic formulas,

and wild experiments

that will delight your friends,

intimidate your enemies, and

impress even grown-ups. But you

can handle it because ...

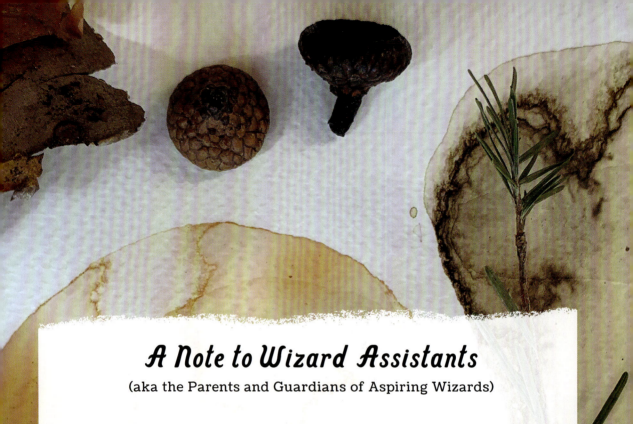

A Note to Wizard Assistants
(aka the Parents and Guardians of Aspiring Wizards)

As an assistant to an aspiring wizard, it's your job to make space for the magic to happen. So...

Be prepared. This book is designed so that wizards in training can start making color magic right away with materials so easy to find that some are literally falling from trees. But if you read the first page or two of each section, you'll find helpful fundamentals like safety tips, which materials work best, and how to set up your space for successful experimenting.

Be safe. For younger, wilder, or first-time wizards, I recommend adult supervision. Protective gear is recommended, and activities that require hands-on help are marked with the one- or two-hand symbol (see **Decoding the Secret Activity Symbols**, p. 11). But beyond these specific notes, it's best to set up a tool kit, workspace, and foraging area with an eye to safety, which may be of only passing interest to the fearless wizard you're assisting.

Save your money. In support of inexpensive, DIY magic, the activities and recipes in this book call for supplies that can be found easily outdoors and in refrigerators. The one thing you might splurge on is good watercolor paper or rice paper. Really, any paper that is well made will support the complexity of natural color. To save money, you can cut large sheets of paper into small squares and have a pile of cheaper or recycled test sheets on hand.

Be adventuresome. You probably want your wizard to find what they seek, and make that perfect blue color that you saw on p. 94, all before lunchtime. But who are you to decide if an experiment is perfect? You can help your wizard follow the rules, but keep in mind that the path to real magic is not straight but winding and full of fruitful cul-de-sacs.

Take a picture. Unless you have a photographic memory, a picture can be a great way to capture these moments (and make your wizard's friends want to join in the fun).

Give yourself permission to be imperfect. If you skip a step somewhere and wind up finger painting with the beet juice on your plate, you might have just stumbled upon some powerful magic yourself.

What Kind of Wizard Are You Today?

As you prepare for adventure, why not use this handy quiz to find out what kind of wizard you are today? Get a sheet of paper, and for each number, write down the letter that is truest about you. Then turn the page.

1. I'm happiest when...
- **A** Digging things up
- **B** Stirring things up
- **C** Explaining things
- **D** Heating things up
- **E** All of the above

2. My favorite tools are...
- **A** A shovel and an old satchel
- **B** Bottles and containers
- **C** Flags and paper airplanes
- **D** Stoves and BBQs
- **E** All of the above

3. My favorite part of myself is...
- **A** My feet
- **B** My spit
- **C** My dreams
- **D** My fingers
- **E** All of the above

4. My favorite question is...
- **A** How?
- **B** What?
- **C** Why?
- **D** When?
- **E** All of the above

5. My favorite kinds of places are...
- **A** Hills, caves, and piles of rock
- **B** Lakes, rivers, and mud puddles
- **C** Tree branches, bleachers, and tall buildings
- **D** Kitchens, grills, and fire pits
- **E** All of the above

6. I've been called...
- **A** Messy
- **B** Nerdy
- **C** Spacey
- **D** Rebellious
- **E** All of the above

Now Find Your Wizard Element!

If you selected...

Mostly A's

You are an **Earth Wizard**. Earth Wizards can discover whole worlds right at their feet. Your object is the spade. Your animal is the worm.

Mostly C's

You are an **Air Wizard**. Air Wizards find magic by looking up and shouting their spells into the wind. Your object is the flag. Your animal is the owl.

Mostly B's

You are a **Water Wizard**. Water Wizards use all kinds of liquids to make colors and don't mind the rain at all. Your object is the glass bottle. Your animal is the rainbow trout.

Mostly D's

You are a **Fire Wizard**. Fire wizards are hard to satisfy, which is why they love to see things change, and they are a little bit dangerous. Your object is the wand. Your animal is the firefly.

Mostly E's

You are a **Rainbow Wizard**. Rainbow wizards are brave, curious, and always changing. Your object is the prism. Your animal is the peacock spider.

To figure out your full wizard classification:

*Add your name + the number of activities from this book you've completed (that's your level number) + your favorite color. For example, you might be known as "Annie, the Level 4 Silver Earth Wizard" or "Soren, the Level 0 Purple Water Wizard." This formula also works for wizard assistants. Ask yours. Who knows, they might surprise you by being a Level 30 White Fire Wizard Assistant. Also note that your wizard type may change from day to day or hour to hour. Then again, it might just last your whole life. If you like, note your wizard type in your notebook (see **Make Your Own Wizard's Notebook**, p. 22). And as you leaf through this book, pay special attention to the activities that are marked with your wizard icon.*

A Special Note to Young Wizards

Following the ancient three-step process of color wizardry, this book is divided into three sections: GATHER, TRANSFORM, and SHARE. Gather is about finding natural tools, materials, and mysterious ingredients. The activities in this section will send you searching for color in leafy forests, seaweedy beaches, berry-stained back alleys, mysterious city parks, and even the dark corners of your fridge. After gathering, you'll learn how to transform your ingredients into color brews—from the boldest black to the palest pink. And finally, you'll share your discoveries with friends, family, and the whole color-hungry human race.

As you go deeper into this book, you will meet some of the powerful (and often forgotten) **Color Wizards of History**, like the woman who figured out how to use the end of the rainbow to fix people's eyes and cell phones (p. 104). Observant wizards will also uncover some astounding **True Magic** facts, like how dying stars made barns red (p. 84).

You can read each section in order, or if you prefer to forge your own path, use this guide like a cookbook and jump right into a color recipe. For independent-minded wizards who don't mind doing a bit of fiddling, there is a universal recipe for making color (p. 54) that works with all kinds of colorful natural objects. And if you get lost, there's also an index at the back.

Decoding the Secret Activity Symbols

 Beginner

 Intermediate

 Advanced

 Expert

 Adult guidance recommended

 Adult assistance required

 Brews overnight

 Outside activity

 Works best in a group

 Recommended for Earth Wizards

 Recommended for Water Wizards

 Recommended for Air Wizards

 Recommended for Fire Wizards

 Recommended for Rainbow Wizards

The Seven Laws of Safe Sorcery

Wizards are a wild, powerful, and sometimes unpredictable folk, which is why the Seven Laws of Safe Sorcery were created hundreds of years ago. Those foolish enough to purposefully ignore the Laws risk having their wizard license revoked or becoming warlocks.

1. **Read carefully.** Any good wizard will tell you that when you miss a step or forget the right incantation, you can end up turning your friend into a cat by mistake. The same goes for color magic. Make sure you have the right tools and ingredients for each activity, follow the instructions, and get inventive only after you fully understand how it works.

2. **Dress for adventure.** When you're outside, bring along a watch, an assistant, sun protection, and clothes for unexpected weather, plus water and snacks (see p. 16). Indoors, you should wear old clothes and a lab coat or smock and have cleanup and safety gear at the ready (see pp. 48–49).

3. **Treat your tools with respect.** Knives and scissors are sharp, stoves are hot, and glass can break. Wizards live a long time because they are slow and watchful and use their powers and tools wisely.

Beware of poison ivy!

4. **Treat nature with respect.** Mushrooms, berries, and leaves can be poisonous, and some plants are rare and need to be protected. Avoid disturbing any bugs, delicate plants, or wild animals. Follow the instructions in regard to natural materials, and if you aren't sure about something you find, don't touch it.

5. **Don't eat your supplies.** There are all kinds of fruits and vegetables that make good art supplies. But never put anything in your mouth that didn't come from a grocery store or that you aren't sure about.

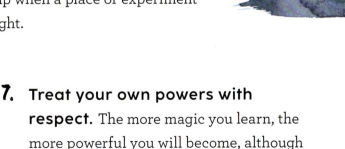

6. **When in doubt, ask your assistant or a wise adult.** A true wizard never stops asking questions and isn't afraid to speak up and get help when a place or experiment doesn't feel right.

7. **Treat your own powers with respect.** The more magic you learn, the more powerful you will become, although you should still avoid turning your friend into a cat.

Investigate mud puddles and hilltops, berry-stained back alleys and unexplored parks. Color is hiding everywhere! Gather your tools, suit up, and go on foraging quests.

Tool Up for Outdoor Adventure

(for indoor setup, see p. 48)

1. HAT A broad brim keeps the sun and rain off, and bonus points if the hat is pointy— a shape perfected by witches for focusing the magic from your head to the sky.

2. CLOAK Dress in layers to be ready for any kind of weather— bonus points for a mysterious hood.

3. WAND Comes in all sizes and style variations, including walking sticks and staffs as well as pens and paintbrushes (See p. 29.)

4. BOOTS Good for muddy or thorny adventuring

5. PLAN or MAP Start somewhere near your house. Obey the signs. Check **The Color Quests** (p. 34) for ideas.

6. SATCHEL Great for storing foraged finds, snacks, and water. (See p. 18 for packing instructions.)

7. BEARD (optional) Long gray beards are kind of itchy, and most kids have difficulty growing them. But they do suggest both knowledge and stealth, two qualities you will find essential.

8. EYES Always open! (See **How to Look Good: The Shrimp and the Hula-Hoop,** p. 26.)

A mint tin makes a great collector's box.

Assemble an Adventure-Worthy Color Wizard's Satchel

TIME: 5–20 minutes

In their own workshops, wizards have all kinds of potions, powders, bottles, cauldrons, spell books, and strange tools. Out in the wilderness (or your local park), it's much better to travel light. In fact, the experienced wizard will often carry only three things with them (plus snacks, of course). See if you can find one item from each of these lists in your home— or borrow them from a friend.

SUPPLY LIST

★ An old backpack or easy-to-carry bag

★ One item from each of the following categories:

NOTICING
Nature books
Notebook and pencil
Map of the area
Binoculars
Magnifying glass

COLLECTING
Pruning shears
Scissors
Trowel
Tweezers
Gardening gloves

STORING
Ziplock bags
Plastic grocery bags
Glass jar or bottle with a tight-fitting lid
Sharpie and blank label

INSTRUCTIONS

1. Start with a backpack or sturdy bag that's easy to carry and that you don't mind getting dirty. In fact, the older and grubbier it looks, the more wizardly it will be.

2. Do a bit of rummaging for items from the supply list that suit your adventure or mood. Put the three most promising items in your satchel. Try to resist adding too much extra stuff, because the less you bring, the more room you'll have for the exciting foraged items you'll discover.

3. Put your packed wizard satchel by the door. You are now ready for adventure!

MORE MAGIC

If you are doing a lot of foraging, you may want to customize your satchel. Try pinning on a ribbon, sewing on a piece of hand-dyed cloth, or ironing on a cool patch. Your decoration can be your favorite color or your wizard element (see **What Kind of Wizard Are You Today?** on p. 7).

Take Note: A Wizard's Notebook

A secret recipe that you never write down will eventually become secret even to you. Keeping your own Wizard's Notebook organizes your thoughts and ideas, so future you can look back at the fascinating beginning of your quest for color. If you are looking for inspiration, **Shěn Kuò** (p. 24), **Sir Isaac Newton** (p. 70), *and* **Emily Dickinson** (p. 105) *all filled their notebooks with ideas that would end up changing the world.*

Make Your Own Wizard's Notebook

TIME: 5 minutes + 20 minutes for decorating

Share this top-secret info with only your most trusted wizard friends—it's more fun to make your own notebook at home than it is to buy one at a store.

SUPPLY LIST

- ★ 10 sheets of paper (letter size) that you can write or draw on
- ★ 1 sheet of thicker paper, cardboard, or card stock for the cover (letter size or a bit larger)
- ★ A decently boingy medium-size rubber band

INSTRUCTIONS

1. Fold each sheet of paper in half like a birthday card.

2. Tuck each folded sheet of paper into the one before so that all the folds line up together like a booklet.

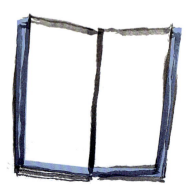

3. Fold the thicker cover paper over all the other nested sheets of paper to form your book.

4. Hold the sheets together with a medium-size elastic band looped around the seam where they fold together. Ten sheets of paper will make a forty-page book!

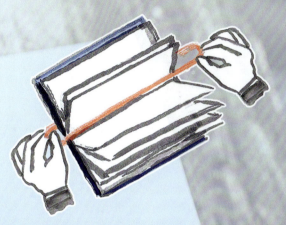

5. Decorate your notebook (see p. 25 for some ideas).

MORE MAGIC

Once you see how easy it is to make your own notebook, you may want to make several: one for color tests, one for gluing in plant specimens, and one for writing up your observations. You can also combine multiple notebooks into one by using a larger rubber band to hold together the bundles.

Making your own notebook is easy and inexpensive, but if you decide to buy one, here are a few recommendations.

The ideal Wizard's Notebook has:

- ★ Paper that's thick enough for you to paint on with watery colors

- ★ Blank pages, lined pages, or graph paper—pick your favorite (see **Make Your Own Wizard's Notebook**, p. 22)

- ★ A smallish size, so you can take your notebook wherever you go

- ★ Pages that open flat so they won't flap around too much in the wind

- ★ A sturdy design (thread-bound with a waterproof hardcover is ideal)

- ★ A reasonable price, because you might end up buying more than one

COLOR HERO:
Real-Life Wizard Shěn Kuò (沈括)

Not only was Shěn Kuò one of the earliest people to explain how rainbows work, but he also made discoveries about music, art, rocks, outer space, and the laws of the universe and wrote it all down in his notebook. Because he was interested in so many different things, he was known as "the first Renaissance man," owing to the fact that he was born nearly one thousand years ago! (That's five hundred years before Leonardo da Vinci.) His observations and notes were put together in a totally wizardly sounding book called *The Dream Pool Essays* (梦溪笔谈), which includes some fantastic descriptions of rainbows.

MAKE EACH NOTEBOOK UNIQUE BY TRYING A FEW OF THE FOLLOWING IDEAS:

★ Add a sticker with your wizard name and email on it. (This is a critical step for wizards young and old who occasionally lose things.)

★ Use lined paper, graph paper, construction paper, watercolor paper, or mix them together (see p. 5 for a note on buying quality paper).

★ Give it a creative title, like *The Secret Color Experiments of Maggie the Aspiring Wizard*.

★ Add stick-on jewels or other cover decorations.

★ Use an old-fashioned date stamper inside to mark significant observations.

★ Make your cover look old by brushing on some coffee or tea, wrapping it in boiled onion skins overnight, or squeezing some lemon on it.

How to Look Good: The Shrimp and the Hula-Hoop

TIME: 15 minutes

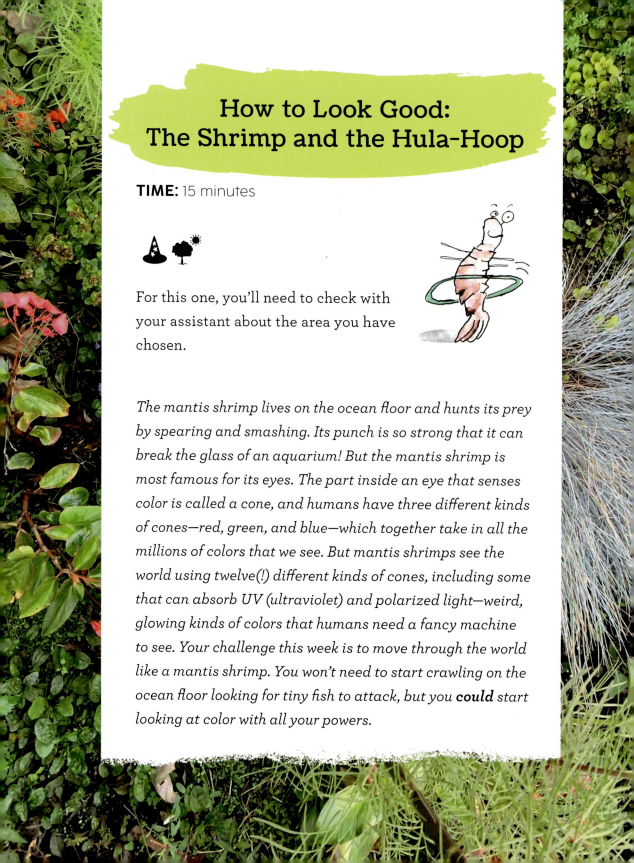

For this one, you'll need to check with your assistant about the area you have chosen.

*The mantis shrimp lives on the ocean floor and hunts its prey by spearing and smashing. Its punch is so strong that it can break the glass of an aquarium! But the mantis shrimp is most famous for its eyes. The part inside an eye that senses color is called a cone, and humans have three different kinds of cones—red, green, and blue—which together take in all the millions of colors that we see. But mantis shrimps see the world using twelve(!) different kinds of cones, including some that can absorb UV (ultraviolet) and polarized light—weird, glowing kinds of colors that humans need a fancy machine to see. Your challenge this week is to move through the world like a mantis shrimp. You won't need to start crawling on the ocean floor looking for tiny fish to attack, but you **could** start looking at color with all your powers.*

SUPPLY LIST

- ★ A small, safe (seemingly boring) outdoor space

- ★ A Hula-Hoop or a piece of string (about 10 feet/3 meters long) stretched out to form a rough circle about the size of a Hula-Hoop

- ★ A notebook and pen

TRUE MAGIC: People with Superpowered Eyes

Humans can see about a million different colors using the three types of cones in their eyes, but there are a few rare people called *tetrachromats* who have four types of cones, which lets them see one hundred million colors!

INSTRUCTIONS

1. Find a safe location outside where you can be a mantis shrimp. This could be a field, a forest, your backyard, or a city square. Don't forget to bring your Hula-Hoop (or string) along with a pen and notebook.

2. Pick a spot. This can be an area with an interesting plant or rock, or you can roll your Hula-Hoop and let it pick its own spot to land.

3. Write the numbers 1 to 13 in your notebook with space after each number.

4. Imagine that you are a mantis shrimp who can see things no other creature can. Look very carefully at what's inside your circle. Instead of touching things, walk around the outside of the circle and forage only with your super-shrimp eyes.

5. Use your numbered list to write down at least 13 things you find in your circle. This can include colors, shapes, textures, and surprising discoveries. Bonus points if you draw one or two of your favorite discoveries. How does it feel to be inside the eyes of a mantis shrimp?

A Wand from the Wild Woods

Did you ever go for a walk and, without really noticing it, find yourself with a stick in your hand? You may have stumbled upon a magic stick. Color wizards will sometimes pick up a random stick that they like the look of, but more often, they are looking for either a *staff* or a *wand* (you will probably want one of each).

A *staff* is a stick used for walking and keeping your balance on your meandering foraging adventures as well as for poking around in the dirt and leaves. For this sort of stick, you want a sturdy one that's about your own height, fits easily in your hand, and looks like it could shoot lightning bolts or at least glow when monsters are near. For a *wand* (which is smaller), read on . . .

Make a Wizard's Paintbrush Wand

TIME: 30–120 minutes

Like larger wizards' staffs, a paintbrush wand connects the world's magic to the magic inside of YOU. The marks that you and this wand make together might just become your secret signature.

SUPPLY LIST

- ★ For the handle: twigs, sticks, or other sturdy, wand-shaped natural materials
- ★ For the bristles: dried grasses, flowers, seed heads, or pine needles
- ★ Tape (masking, duct, or other waterproof tape)
- ★ Ink or watery paint
- ★ Plastic tray (a take-out container works well)
- ★ Lots of paper
- ★ Scissors

TRUE MAGIC: The World's Oldest Stick

Sticks have been around for as long as trees have, more than one hundred million years before the dinosaurs, but the oldest-ever "more than just a stick" was found in a remote place in Germany, and the scientist who found it was pretty sure it was used as a throwing spear to ambush prey about 400,000 years ago.

INSTRUCTIONS

1. **Forage for a wand.** This will be the handle of your paintbrush. Usually, brush handles are about the size of a pencil (7½ inches/ 19 centimeters), straight, and strong, with a bit of flexibility. But spend some time finding a stick that looks magic to your eyes and feels magic in your hands. If you are having trouble deciding, choose wood that (a) has fallen from a tree that is special to you, (b) is from a place that you love, or (c) belongs to your birth tree (see below).

2. **Forage for the bristles.** The bristles form the end of the brush that you will dip into the ink or paint. Go outside into your backyard, the green space along the sidewalk, or the nearest park. Can you find

MORE MAGIC

If you are still having trouble finding a wand, you might consider looking for a stick from your birth tree. Find your birth tree on this list passed down from the Celts, an ancient people who lived in the areas we now call Britain and France and were famous for their tree-worshipping wizards called Druids.

December 24– January 20
Birch

January 21– February 17
Rowan

February 18– March 17
Ash

March 18– April 14
Alder

April 15– May 12
Willow

May 13– June 9
Hawthorn

June 10– July 7
Oak

any seed heads, thick grasses, or pine needles? Imagine what kind of mark each one would make if it were used as a paintbrush. Carefully put the most interesting finds into your wizard's satchel, and when you get home, lay out all the options on a table and pick the one you think might make an interesting pattern.

3. **Attach your chosen bristles to your chosen wand.** Line up your stick and your bristles so they overlap, and then wrap tape around their meeting point. Wind the tape around four or five times, or until it's all securely attached.

4. **Ink your brush.** Pour some black ink or watery paint (see **Dark Wizard Ink**, p. 112) into the plastic tray and dip the tip of your magic paintbrush into the liquid.

5. **Make your mark.** Test out your brush on paper by (a) dragging it across the paper in straight lines, (b) making curvy paths from one corner to another, (c) making fast, messy scribbles in the middle of the page (see **Genius Squiggles**, p. 109), (d) making big, slow loops to cover the whole paper, or (e) (really the best test) just going wild with it.

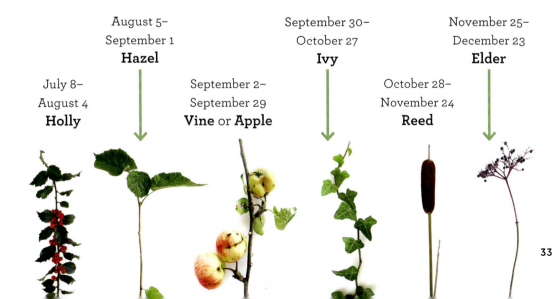

July 8–
August 4
Holly

August 5–
September 1
Hazel

September 2–
September 29
Vine or **Apple**

September 30–
October 27
Ivy

October 28–
November 24
Reed

November 25–
December 23
Elder

The Color Quests:
Hunt for Hidden Color

For Each Quest

TIME: 30–120 minutes

SUPPLY LIST

- ★ An assistant
- ★ A wizard's satchel or bag (see p. 18)
- ★ Snacks and water
- ★ One of the four Color Quest lists (bring this book or take a picture of the page you need)
- ★ Your Wizard's Notebook (p. 21) and a pencil

INSTRUCTIONS

1. Choose one of the adventures on the following pages. Talk to your assistant about where you will adventure and how long it might last.

2. Keep your eyes open (see **How to Look Good: The Shrimp and the Hula-Hoop**, p. 26).

3. Bring your wizard's satchel, and don't forget to pack snacks and water.

4. Try to check off as many things as you can find from the list for each quest—but bring home just two or three.

5. Keep track of your favorite discoveries in your Wizard's Notebook.

6. You can use your finds to make a color using **The Color Wizard's Secret Guide to Making Color from Practically Anything** (p. 54). There are also suggested recipes next to some of the list items that follow.

THE RULES

1. The quest is up to you. A quest can be a short trip to a local park, a weekend camping, an outing with all your friends, or even your fifteen-minute walk home from school over the course of a week. If you are in a particularly magical place, you might want to look for stuff from all the lists. Or make your own quest with a map and challenging finds for friends.

2. Be careful. Talk over the Color Quest with your assistant. Follow the **Seven Laws of Safe Sorcery** (see p. 10) and make sure you have permission to forage in the area. Avoid poisonous plants and berries—if you aren't sure whether something is toxic, leave it be. Oh, and never wake a sleeping dragon.

3. Take only what you need. Don't take a plant that you see only one of, and never take the whole plant. Finding something doesn't mean you have to put it in your satchel—drawing a find in your book or marking it on a map for future adventures is just as good for your wizard training.

QUEST 1
Wild Waters

Wander with an adult alongside rivers, lakes, ocean beaches, ponds, or mysterious mud puddles. Bring along a container with a lid.

 Don't go in or near water alone.

- seaweed or pond plants
- soft rocks (try scraping them across a flat rock or pavement—if they leave a mark, they are soft)
- white shell
- colorful sand
- sparkly shell (see **Make Your Own Sidewalk Chalk**, p. 137)
- blue shell
- pink shell
- purple shell
- driftwood
- dark, nonpoisonous berries (see **Indigo Berry Blast Blobs**, p. 98)
- cold campfire ash (see **Dark Wizard Ink**, p. 112)
- blue rock
- water from a stream
- water from a magical pond
- water from a fountain
- driftwood wand (see **Make a Wizard's Paintbrush Wand**, p. 30)
- driftwood stirring stick
- floating nut
- floating pine cone
- an interesting piece of ice (see **Roads of Blood**, p. 81)

QUEST 2
Enchanted Earth

Uncover rocky paths, piles of sand, a garden (with permission), or a dusty schoolyard. Dress to get dirty.

- red dirt
- yellow dirt
- brown dirt
- gray dirt
- orange-colored root
- dandelion flower
- goldenrod flower
- green grass
- sparkly rock
- crumbly green rock
- soft red rock (try scraping it across a flat rock or pavement—if it leaves a mark, it's soft)
- soft brown rock
- soft yellow rock
- soft rock of any other color
- ferns (see **Natural Spray Paint**, p. 142)
- lichen (taken only from fallen branches)
- sand
- fallen branch wand (see **Make a Wizard's Paintbrush Wand**, p. 30)
- orange flowers
- barberry
- bark (see **Silvery Acorn Cap Ink**, p. 116)

And if you have access to a garden:

- rosemary
- marigold flowers
- madder
- daylilies
- sunflowers
- rose petals

QUEST 3
Color Falling from the Sky

Explore deep forests, park bushes, and tree-lined streets. Watch for falling nuts!

- colorful leaves of any kind (see **Natural Confetti**, p. 151)
- really green leaf (see **Green Glow-in-the-Dark Plant Energy**, p. 91)
- orange leaf
- yellow leaf
- golden leaf
- brown leaf
- purple leaf
- gray leaf
- pink bark
- red bark
- pine cone
- acorn (see **Silvery Acorn Cap Ink**, p. 116)
- black walnut
- chestnut
- other kinds of nuts
- oak galls
- purple berries (do not eat)
- black berries (do not eat)
- apple tree leaves or bark
- pink peppercorns
- alder cones
- fallen red flower petals
- fallen blue flower petals
- hibiscus flowers
- cherries (see **Indigo Berry Blast Blobs**, p. 98)
- eucalyptus leaves (do not feed to your pet)
- fallen twig covered in lichen
- fern (see **Natural Spray Paint**, p. 142)
- oak leaf

QUEST 4
The Supernatural World

Discover the unexpected in the places where humans and nature meet, like sidewalks, alleyways, chain-link fences, and even your own kitchen. Beware of sharp objects and NO TRESPASSING signs.

- bricks
- copper penny (pre-1982) or other penny (see **Copper Penny Blue Ink**, p. 95)
- rusty objects that aren't sharp (for all rusty finds, see **Make a Martian Landscape**, p. 83)
- railway spike
- purple berry (do not eat)
- wild grape (do not eat)
- grapevines (see **How to Make Vine Charcoal for Ink or Drawing**, p. 110)
- other woody vines
- piece of chalk
- chunk of drywall
- charred wood
- cold coals from a fire or BBQ
- yellow onion skins
- red onion skins
- avocado pits
- black beans
- coffee or coffee grounds
- tea or tea bag

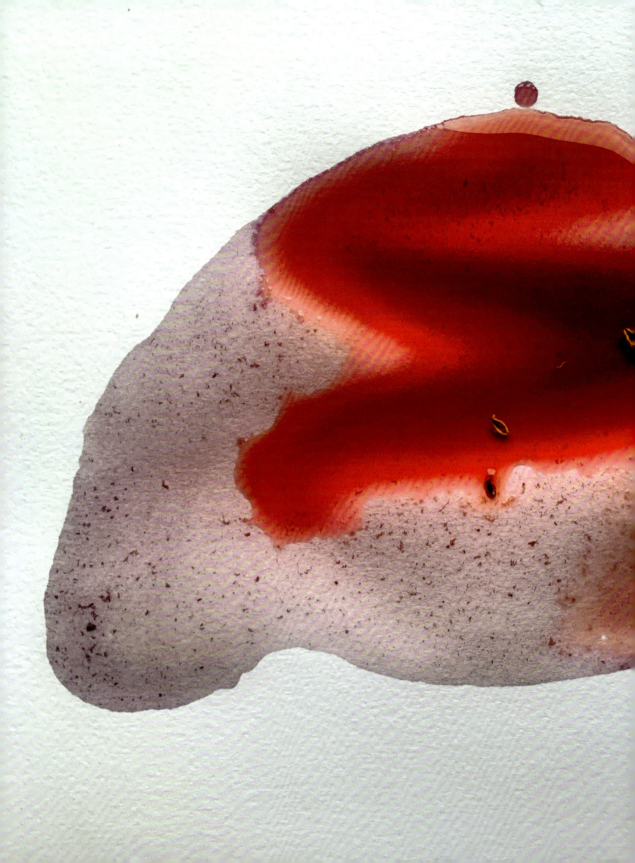

Transform!

Get ready to mix, cook, grind, and refine your gathered materials into something entirely new. If you are the sort of color wizard who likes a good potion, then take off your cape, set your satchel down, and prepare your space for some mad wizardly experiments, because this section is filled with magical alchemy.

How to (Temporarily) Turn Your Kitchen into a Secret Laboratory for Mad Wizardly Experiments

TIME: 15–45 minutes

Your kitchen probably has water, a stove, a flat space for working, glass containers, and maybe an old beet in the fridge. You'll be surprised by how much you can do with just those basics. Look even closer, and hidden away in the kitchen cupboards, you'll find many of the tools and ingredients you need for magic. So, before you ask your assistant to buy anything for color making, have a look at this diagram and set up your kitchen lab accordingly. Even though you are a mad scientist/sorcerer, for color experiments, you will find that a clean, well-organized lab is better for magic than a messy space.

1. PERMISSION
Locate and talk to the boss of your kitchen. Make sure they know what you are up to and confirm that the space is free and that they can assist you (if needed). If they need more convincing, tell them that you are "doing important scientific work" and that you are "promoting them to the title of Lab Manager."

2. A FLAT SURFACE
Choose a spot that is cleared off and separate from food preparation. Cover your work area with newspapers or a washable covering. Before you start a recipe, collect all the ingredients you will need. A well-organized work area lets you really go wild in your experiments.

THE WIZARDLY KITCHEN-LAB

3. CLEANUP and SAFETY SUPPLIES

Have a sponge, soapy water, and paper towels at the ready. A lab coat or smock plus safety googles and gloves come in handy too.

7. THE SPICE RACK

Check here for turmeric, paprika, whole cloves, alum (see **The Color Wizard's Secret Guide to Making Color from Practically Anything**, p. 54), and any other brightly colored spices.

6. THE CUPBOARD

If you do some foraging, you will most likely be able to find a measuring cup and spoons, bowls, an old pot, a wooden spoon or other stirrer, a strainer, a funnel, ziplock bags, coffee filters, empty plastic take-out containers, and empty jars and bottles.

4. THE STOVE

When using the stove (or microwave), make sure you have adult supervision. It's great to have a special pot just for color making.

8. EMPTY SHELF

Talk with the Lab Manager about clearing a little area for you in the fridge and/or in that cupboard that's full of containers with lids that don't fit.

5. THE BAKING DRAWER

You will find that salt, baking soda, cornstarch, sugar, and vinegar all have magic powers.

9. THE FRIDGE

Look carefully here for lemons, beets, red onions, carrots, and any brightly colored juices. You may also want to keep some natural inks here (if you are allowed).

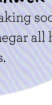

Natural inks make a great stain for wood and string.

See-Through Sorcery

Five Cool Things Made from Glass That Are Great for Color Experiments

Did you ever wonder why wizards and mad scientists have so many vials and test tubes and strange bottles bubbling away in their laboratory? Well, glass is nonreactive (which means chemicals can't wreck it), it comes in all kinds of weird shapes for different kinds of experiments, and it's easy to clean. And most importantly, it's clear, so you can watch when your potion bubbles, changes color, or does something else that's cool.

1. MEASURING CUP almost unbreakable • includes measurements • microwavable • pourable

2. BEAKER good for measuring, heating up, and pouring • comes in lots of different sizes

3. ERLENMEYER FLASK

hard to tip over • includes measurements • easy to swirl around without spilling • strong

4. DROPPER

(sometimes called a pipette) great for measuring small amounts • fun and easy for smaller hands to use • sciencey-looking • less messy when mixing • drops look cool on paper

5. INK BOTTLE

great for storage • easy to carry on Color Quests • almost unbreakable • includes a built-in dropper

The Color Wizard's Secret Guide to Making Color from Practically Anything

TIME: 30–120 minutes (includes foraging time)

*This recipe is not for everyone, but . . . if you already have a satchel full of something interesting, your kitchen is set up to experiment, and your assistant is on hand, you just might want to start by understanding the basics of inventing your own color of paint. I can't tell you what color you are going to get, and it might not be what you expect, but I **can** promise that there will be some mysterious smells, some bubbling pots, and in the end, a bottle of color that only YOU could have made.*

SUPPLY LIST

- ½ cup of any *one* of the ingredients from **The Color Quests** (see p. 34). The quests offer easy-to-find sources of color, but anything natural and nonpoisonous with a bright color is worth a try.
- Bowl
- 1 cup water
- An old pot
- Strainer or coffee filter
- Funnel
- A glass jar or bottle, sterilized with boiling water by your assistant or run through a dishwasher, and a tight-fitting lid
- Gum arabic (available online or at most art supply stores)
- Whole clove or one drop of wintergreen oil (optional)
- Blank sticker to label your ink (optional)
- Alum, a pickling salt found in the spice section (optional)

INSTRUCTIONS

1. **Collect:** Choose and find your secret color ingredient. For best results, stick to one color source per recipe.

2. **Sort:** Separate the most colorful parts from the less colorful parts of your secret ingredient.

3. **Process:** Crush, grind, carefully cut into tiny pieces, or squeeze your ingredient (if it's juicy) into a bowl.

4. **Brew:** With the help of your assistant, add your smushed-up color to one cup of water in an old pot, and boil it until your liquid is reduced by half (don't burn it). For very juicy berries, you may be able to skip this step.

5. **Strain:** Pour your liquid into a strainer or coffee filter that fits into your funnel, and drip it into your glass jar.

6. **Bind:** Add 1 dropper (about 10 drops) of gum arabic to your mixture. This binds the color to the water.

7. **Protect:** Put one whole clove or one drop of wintergreen oil in as a preservative (optional), or keep your natural color in the fridge.

8. **Decorate:** If you want, you can put a sticker on your ink bottle and label it with a name (see p. 131).

TROUBLESHOOTING

Put a drop or two of your color on a piece of thick white paper and wait for it dry. If the color is too light, try adding more of the color ingredient or boiling the mixture for longer. If it's too thick, add a little water, and if it's too thin, add some gum arabic. Adding ½ tsp of alum to the water may brighten yellow ingredients. If it smells weird, a drop of wintergreen oil or a whole clove will help. Don't forget to record your successes (and beautiful failures) in your Wizard's Notebook (see p. 22).

MORE MAGIC

To get a small, dry watercolor palette, you can fill a bottle cap with your color and let it dry for a few days. Six of these bottle caps fit nicely into a mints tin. Dip a wet brush in to rewet the paint when you're ready to use it. To make your paint a little thicker, use a bit of gum arabic, honey, or cornstarch. Adding a thickener also helps natural paint or ink stick for potato prints (see **Say It with Potatoes**, p. 140).

On Drying Time

Unlike many of the paints, inks, and markers you get at the dollar store, natural ink has no chemicals in it to make it dry faster. So after you test things out on paper, you might have to go get some lunch and then come back to see how your tests are coming along. You may even have to leave your art overnight. You can ask your assistant to keep a space open for your drying work and explain to them that three of your magical ingredients are air (or oxygen), time, and patience. Often, the longer you wait, the more magic secretly happens between the paper and the color.

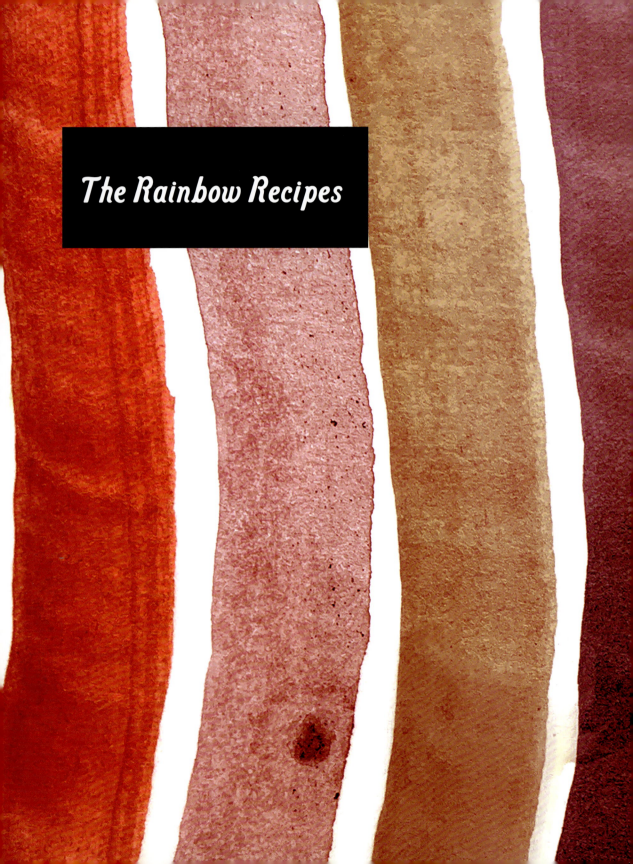

Find a Rainbow in the Dark

TIME: 5 minutes (+ one full night's sleep to think about how amazing it is)

It's time to make your own rainbow. The great light-splitting wizard Sir Isaac Newton (see p. 70) did this experiment before flashlights were invented. He poked a hole through his window screen to get a straight beam of light, directed it through a special piece of glass called a prism, and found his rainbow. His spell was a bit different, but the magic is the same. Here's your chance to uncover all the different colors that have been hiding inside ordinary light, just waiting for you to find them.

SUPPLY LIST

- ★ A clear, round-rimmed water glass or glass container (a coffee carafe works especially well)
- ★ Water
- ★ A low table or work surface
- ★ A dark room with an empty wall
- ★ A flashlight (incandescent, not LED)

INSTRUCTIONS

1. Fill your glass almost totally full with water and place it on a table near an empty wall. Be careful not to spill it.

2. Hold the flashlight right up to the glass and shine it at an angle through the glass. Watch where the light goes.

3. As you move the flashlight around and change the angle of the beam of light, you should see the colors of a rainbow forming on the wall.

4. That's it. You made white light show its true colors! Can you count all seven of them?

TROUBLESHOOTING

If you are having trouble finding the rainbow, try shining the flashlight up through the water or at an angle down toward the table. Depending on the size of your flashlight and glass, it might be easier to form a rainbow on the ceiling or the table rather than the wall. Because you are curving light (which is kind of a superpower), your rainbow might be a bit sneaky, but after a few minutes of playing with it, you should be able to find the perfect angle to form some beautiful colors.

MORE MAGIC

Add some food coloring to your container of water. What happens to the rainbow? Try lining up bottles of different colors of ink in the beam of the flashlight. How does that change your rainbow? What happens if you use a differently shaped glass? Try adding this experiment to **The Psychedelic Sorcerer's Disco Party** (see p. 148).

Take the Rainbow for a Walk

TIME: 30–40 minutes

In the last experiment, you found a rainbow in the dark by breaking up light. Now it's time to make one by mixing.

SUPPLY LIST

- ★ A clean workspace protected by newspaper, plastic, or a washable covering
- ★ 6 clear cups or glasses (plastic is fine)
- ★ Red, yellow, and blue food coloring (I endorse store-bought here)
- ★ Water
- ★ Stick or spoon for stirring
- ★ 10 pieces of absorbent paper towel
- ★ Scissors

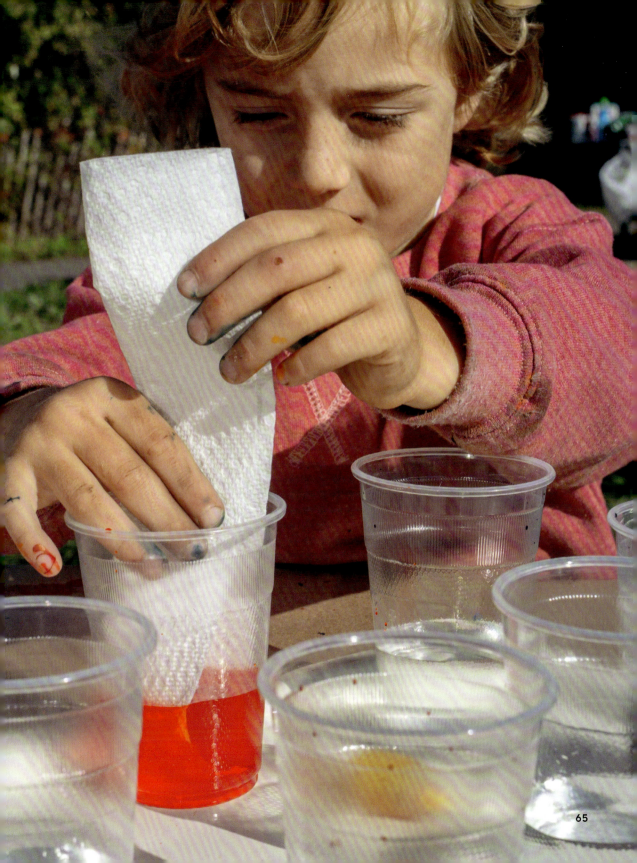

INSTRUCTIONS

1. Begin with 6 clear cups or glasses next to each other, arranged in a circle on your protected workspace.

2. In the first cup, add 7 drops of red food coloring.

3. In the third cup, add 7 drops of yellow food coloring.

4. In the fifth cup, add 7 drops of blue food coloring.

5. Add water only to the cups with food coloring so that they're nearly full. Stir until combined. There should be an empty cup between each colored cup.

6. Prepare your paper towels by folding each lengthwise once, and then again, and then a third time so they form thin strips. Half-size sheets of paper towels need only one or two lengthwise folds.

7. Fold these long strips in half widthwise, and then trim 1 inch (2.5 centimeters) off the end.

8. Tuck the strips between the cups like in the photo. The paper towels should form a low arch from one cup to the next and touch the bottom of both cups without leaving much extra paper. Arranged in a circle, the cups should all have one arched paper towel going in and one going out.

9. The color should start traveling right away. After about 20 minutes, all the cups should be equally full, and you should have a rainbow of colors!

TROUBLESHOOTING

If things aren't moving after a few minutes, try adding more water. If the color is moving very slowly, you may need to try again with a different, more absorbent brand of paper towel.

TRUE MAGIC:
Why the Color Moves

The colored water moves up the paper towel (against gravity) by **capillary action**, the same secret power that allows water to travel from the roots of a tree all the way up to its leaves at the top. Trees have tiny little invisible tunnels that suck water up into the air like a straw. Paper towels (which are made from trees) also have tiny spaces with air that suck up water. The color comes along with the water for the ride. When the paper towel gets totally full of water, gravity takes over, and it starts dripping into the next glass.

MORE MAGIC

The paper towels can be dried and then unfolded to uncover some fantastical patterns. You can reuse them as wrapping paper or pendant flags for **A Rainbow Wizard Birthday** (see p. 150).

MORE TRUE MAGIC:
How to Make New Colors

You started with just three colors, and you made three new ones (plus some in-between colors on the paper towels). The empty glasses are where the colors get to meet and mix. So, when red and yellow come together, they make orange. When yellow and blue come together, they make green. And when blue and red come together, they make purple. Red, yellow, and blue are called the **primary colors**, and they are the most powerful—if you learn how to work with them, they can make all the other visible colors.

EVEN MORE TRUE MAGIC:
Water Is Probably Alien

Water is a magical, clear substance that can change from a cloud to a snowball to liquid in just a few minutes. It also keeps everything on earth alive, makes up most of your body, and is in almost every recipe in this book. So where does this amazing ingredient come from? Scientists are pretty sure that most of Earth's water came from watery space rocks that landed on our planet a few billion years ago.

COLOR HERO:

Sir Isaac Newton

Almost four hundred years ago, Isaac Newton was an isolated kid living on a farm. His dad had died before he was born, and Isaac was supposed to help take care of the sheep and his younger siblings. Instead, he spent a lot of time looking at sunbeams coming through a crack in the door and scribbling notes about what he saw. He wasn't the best student at school, but he had three things going for him—which eventually made him one of the most famous scientists ever. He was (1) curious, (2) a problem solver, and (3) never one to give up. When he couldn't find a good clock for his experiments, he invented one out of water. When he couldn't get a strong enough telescope to see the stars, he made one of the best telescopes in the world. He needed a special kind of metal to do this, so he melted together a few different kinds of metal in his backyard. Isaac's hard work got him accepted into one of the finest schools in England, but while he was there, there was a pandemic, and everyone was sent home.

Now, someone these days might have sat around playing video games, but not Isaac. In lockdown, while everyone was freaking out about the pandemic and fiery balls they'd seen in the sky, Isaac got busy. Looking at the sky with the telescope he designed himself, he saw that the fiery balls were comets, and he also figured out how planets and comets were moving around the sun by inventing a whole new kind of math. He got curious about why apples fall down and not up, and by answering his own question, he uncovered an invisible power that holds the whole universe together, which he called gravity. And (most importantly for us) he closed his door, covered his windows in black, and made a little hole in the black cloth to create a beam of light. In this beam of light he put a piece of cut glass called a prism, which made rainbow patterns on his wall and showed how the clear light we see is actually made up of seven colors.

Because he was doing all kinds of math and formulating ideas about how the world works, we now call him a scientist, but because he was looking at the world in a new way and figuring out how regular things like light and water and fire could do extraordinary things like become a rainbow, tell time, and help people see into outer space, we might also call him a wizard. He certainly was magic. The following is a secret formula that Newton did not make up but that was inspired by his success.

A Formula for Magic, Inspired by Newton

$$(C + P) \times H = \diamondsuit$$

Curiosity (notice everything and ask ANY question that pops into your head) + **P**roblem solving (try different approaches, and if you are missing anything, make it yourself) × **H**ard work (keep going, even if it gets boring or frustrating or people tell you it's impossible) = **The Magic** (totally worth it, may help you change the world)

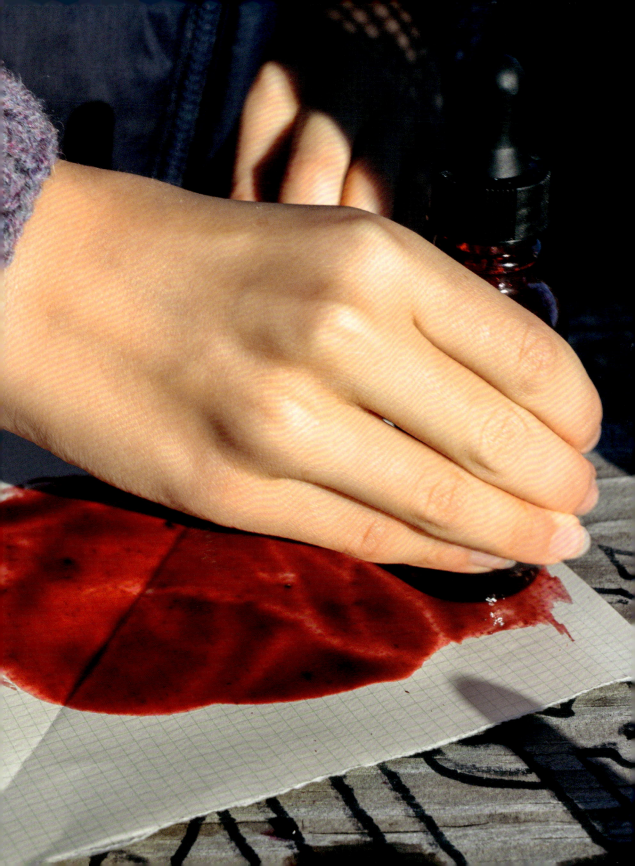

Bubbly, Fiery Dragon's Blood Ink

If you manage to find a real dragon during your color adventures, and for some reason she agrees to let you collect some blood, then all you need to do is put that blood into a fancy bottle. Can't find dragon's blood? This recipe is surprisingly close to the real stuff.

TIME: 30 minutes

SUPPLY LIST

- 2 tablespoons turmeric

- 2 tablespoons baking soda

- 2 small bowls

- Tray (any flat washable surface will work—try a plastic take-out container lid, an old plate, or a baking tray)

- Spoon

- Vinegar, lemon juice, or citric acid (a few tablespoons or more)

- Droppers (also known as pipettes)

- Water

- Small bottle with a lid and label for your ink

INSTRUCTIONS

1. Add the turmeric and baking soda to one of the bowls. Keep mixing them until you notice a color change. This will be your dragon's blood powder.

2. Spread this powder onto your tray with a spoon.

3. Fill the second bowl with vinegar (or lemon juice or citric acid) and drip a full dropper of it on your tray. You can add water as well.

4. Keep mixing and playing until you have just the color you want. Use the dropper to fill your small bottle with this special substance.

TRUE MAGIC: Red Is the First Color That Babies See

When babies are born, everything looks dark or light to them. Within a week, they start noticing the color red. When they're five months old, they can see all the colors of the rainbow.

MORE MAGIC

⚡ Draw a dragon with markers, and then use a paintbrush and your Dragon's Blood Ink to draw some fire.

⚡ Decorate your bottle with stickers and dragon's runes. Dragon's runes look a bit like claw marks, but they are actually a whole language called draconic. Some say that the draconic script was created by Io, the great dragon of magic and knowledge. I'm not an expert in dragon languages—but, at great danger to myself, I did manage to get ahold of this alphabet for you.

The Dragonic Alphabet

A B C D E F G H I J K L M

N O P Q R S T U V W X Y Z

0 1 2 3 4 5 6 7 8 9

Bright-Pink (Underground) Ink

TIME: 30 minutes

They live at the bottom of your fridge. They're hard to cut up. Hard to clean. And to be honest, they taste like dirt. But for the color wizard . . . BEETS ARE YOUR SECRET WEAPON.

SUPPLY LIST

- ★ 3 small whole beets, 3 tablespoons beet powder or beet juice, or the juice from one can of canned beets
- ★ Water
- ★ Strainer or fine sieve
- ★ 1 teaspoon white vinegar or lemon juice
- ★ Bowl
- ★ Brushes, a dropper, or other mark-making tools
- ★ Paper
- ★ Container with a lid for storage

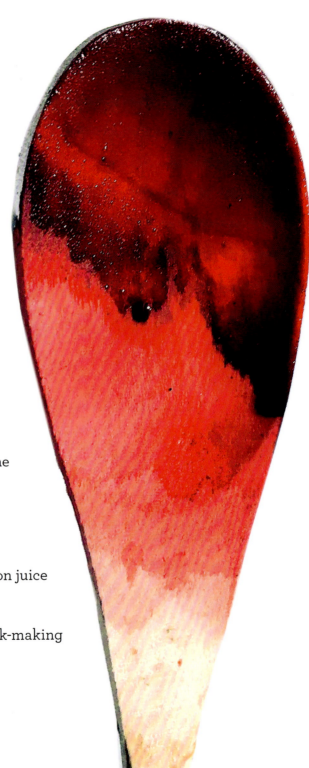

INSTRUCTIONS

1. **Juice:** Choose a method from the list below depending on what sort of beets you have on hand. Make sure to get help from your assistant when cutting, cooking, or using a blender or juicer. No matter your method, you want to end up with a bright-colored juice that has the consistency of a thin syrup.

   → **Raw beets:** First, cut the beets into small pieces. You can liquefy them in a blender on high with ½ cup of water or simmer them on the stove with 1 cup of water until the liquid is a bright magenta color. You can also juice your beet pieces according to the instructions of your juicer.

   → **Beet powder:** Stir 2 tablespoons of beet powder into ½ cup of water.

   → **Canned beets:** Simply remove the whole beets and use the liquid.

   → **Premade beet juice (sometimes called beetroot juice):** This can be found at most health food stores and works great as is!

TRUE MAGIC:
Baby Flamingos Get Their Color from Pink Milk

Both mom and dad flamingos eat a lot of orangey-pink shrimp to make a bright-pink liquid called "crop milk" in their long necks, which they basically barf up to feed their babies. The babies, who are born with gray feathers, slowly get their patented pink flamingo coloring by drinking this milk.

2. **Strain:** If necessary, remove any larger pieces of beet with a fork or spoon, and pour your liquid through a strainer or fine sieve to remove any small beet particles.

3. **Keep it pink:** Add 1 teaspoon of white vinegar or lemon juice to your beet ink. (This will keep it a nice bright pink and act as a preservative.)

4. **Pour:** Take your beet mixture, pour it into a bowl, and dip your brush in.

5. **Test:** Using a brush or dropper, test out your new ink on paper.

6. **Store:** Any leftover beet juice can be bottled and saved. This is one ink recipe that you *can* eat. If you're going to consume it, be sure to store it in a tightly sealed container in the fridge, and use it within a day or two. Otherwise, you should label it as ink—and still store it in the fridge!

TRUE MAGIC: Is It Food or Paint?

While it's smart to keep your food and your paint separate, they may have a few things in common. Scientists are discovering that the same magical ingredients (called phytonutrients) that make natural colors bright also make colorful fruits and vegetables especially healthy. So, if your parents give you some colorful food that you hate the taste of, you can tell them that you need it for your experiments (after having a polite taste or two).

TRUE MAGIC: Roads of Blood

In the winter, salt is often used to melt the ice on roads and sidewalks. Recently, scientists and snow-removal workers have begun experimenting with using the sugars from leftover beets on roads and sidewalks to melt ice instead, because salt can be harmful to plants and animals. It works quite well, but some drivers are a bit shocked to see the drippy beet-colored puddles on the road and sidewalks.

MORE MAGIC

- ⚡ Thinner beet ink works great as fake blood.
- ⚡ Thicker beet ink can even melt ice (see **Roads of Blood**, above).
- ⚡ Put a few dropperfuls of beet ink onto a blank stamp pad, and use a potato carved into a heart shape to make prints for natural tattoos, wrapping paper, and posters.
- ⚡ A few drops of beet juice mixed into white frosting can make pink cupcakes!

Make a Martian Landscape

TIME: Overnight (unless you use the fast method, in which case it takes about 20 minutes)

 Rust will stain some surfaces and you shouldn't pour it down your sink—it's not good for pipes.

Planet Mars is red because of iron. Our planet doesn't look as red because most of Earth's iron is hidden deep within its core, but on Mars the iron is right on the surface. It's windy on Mars, so oxygen gets mixed with iron dust to make—you guessed it—rust. In this activity, you will make a strange alien landscape out of the same stuff, but you won't need a Martian dust storm to do it.

NOTE: If you make a big batch of rust water, it ages well and can be used in **Silvery Acorn Cap Ink**, p. 116.

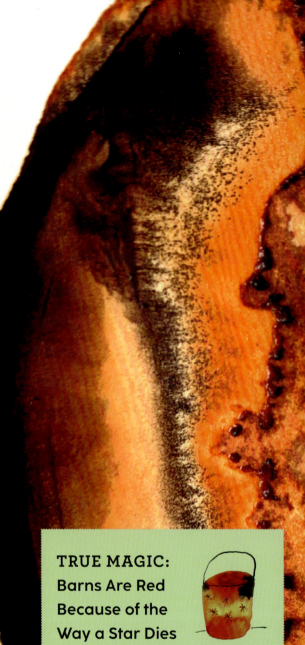

SUPPLY LIST

- ★ A clean workspace protected by newspaper, plastic, or a washable covering
- ★ 2 glass jars—one should be small with a tight-fitting lid
- ★ Enough pieces of rusted material to loosely fill your jar (or for the fast method, fine steel wool, which can be purchased at most hardware stores)
- ★ 2 teaspoons salt
- ★ 2 cups white vinegar
- ★ Metal strainer
- ★ Coffee filter
- ★ Paper towels
- ★ Ink dropper or pipette
- ★ A piece of watercolor paper or other kind of thick paper

INSTRUCTIONS

1. Use your glass jar with a lid to collect some rusty pieces of metal. This adventure is great for city wizards, but bring your

> **TRUE MAGIC: Barns Are Red Because of the Way a Star Dies**
>
>
>
> Yup, iron is the last element that a star makes before it blows up. This means that there is a lot of iron in our solar system, including on Earth, and so the cheapest way to make red paint that really lasts is with iron and oxygen.

assistant along so they can help you carefully harvest your rusty objects. These could be anything metal that has turned an orangey-brown color but that isn't too sharp, such as nuts and bolts, washers, nails, or a link of chain. Be sure to put the lid on your jar before you put it in your pack, as bits of rust can get messy. For wizards in a rush, steel wool in a salt-and-vinegar solution will turn into rust water a lot quicker, although the results may not be quite as wizardly.

MORE MAGIC

Why not make a whole solar system of natural paint planets? Try **Bubbly, Fiery Dragon's Blood Ink** (p. 73) and **Copper Penny Blue Ink** (p. 95). Cut out your planets and hang them with string from two crossed sticks to make a mobile.

2. At home, open your glass jar, add the salt, and completely cover your rust bits in vinegar. Put the lid back on and give the jar a shake.

3. Take the lid off (so it can get lots of air) and leave it overnight, or until the liquid is the color of a nice dark tea. This liquid is called rust water.

4. Pour the rust water through the metal strainer and into the second glass jar, discarding any rusty pieces. Now pour it back into the first jar through the coffee filter to strain out smaller rusty pieces. Wipe up any spills with a paper towel.

5. Use 2 or 3 full ink droppers to make a big puddle of rust water on your paper.

6. Press the bottom of the empty jar into the puddle of rust water on the paper. Enlarge the puddle by twirling your glass jar to make a circular pool of ink. Rinse off the bottom of your jar.

7. Wait for your "iron planet" to dry. (This may take an hour or two.)

Spicy Highlighter Markers

TIME: 20–40 minutes

If you told your friends that you could make a set of markers out of your spice drawer, they probably wouldn't believe you. Wait till you show them these! Spicy markers are great for decorating black-and-white printouts and maps. They're your own personal colors, and they smell interesting (in a good way).

⚠️ Alcohol-based ink can stain wood, countertops, and clothes. You should also avoid contact with your eyes.

SUPPLY LIST

★ A clean workspace protected by newspaper, plastic, or a washable covering

★ Safety goggles

★ 1 cup isopropyl (or rubbing) alcohol (ask your assistant to help you check your medicine cabinet or local pharmacy)

★ 4 small glass beakers or pourable measuring cups

- ★ 1 tablespoon turmeric
- ★ 1 tablespoon paprika
- ★ 1 tablespoon cinnamon
- ★ 1 tablespoon curry powder
- ★ 4 two-inch (5-centimeter) squares of cheesecloth
- ★ String
- ★ 4 empty markers (available online or at art supply stores; refillable bingo daubers also work well)
- ★ Paper, for testing and artwork
- ★ Glass jar with tight-fitting lid, for storage

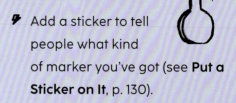

MORE MAGIC

⚡ Add a sticker to tell people what kind of marker you've got (see **Put a Sticker on It**, p. 130).

⚡ Try these alternative pigments in your marker set:

- Beet powder
- Black walnut powder
- Matcha powder
- Saffron (beware—it's expensive!)
- Blue pea flower powder (available online)
- Instant coffee

INSTRUCTIONS

1. Put on your safety goggles to protect your eyes. If you don't have safety goggles, regular swimming goggles will work, too! Isopropyl alcohol will sting if it splashes into your eyes. If that happens, flush the affected eye with lots of room-temperature water.

2. Measure out ¼ cup of isopropyl alcohol into each of the four glass containers.

3. Put a tablespoon of your spice of choice into the middle of one of the squares of cheesecloth and tie it up with the string into a bundle.

4. Dip the bundle into the alcohol until it's submerged.

5. Leave your bundle in the alcohol for 20 minutes, or until you have a nice bright color (you can press down on it with a spoon to get more color out).

6. Pour your alcohol ink into the empty marker and (IMPORTANT) secure the lid.

7. Repeat the process for each of your spice colors.

8. Test them out on paper.

9. Extra marker ink can be stored in a labeled glass jar with a tight-fitting lid.

Green Glow-in-the-Dark Plant Energy

TIME: 1 hour

If plants are magic (and they probably are), then trees are their wizard leaders. Their trunks can lift water hundreds of feet into the air. They feed from their roots, which are even bigger than their branches and have a secret, underground internet (called the "Wood Wide Web") that is powered by fungi and lets them send messages to their tree friends. The leaves of trees clean the air while making a magical substance called oxygen that allows us to breathe. We have trees to thank for pirate ships, chewing gum, paper, rubber, and a whole bunch of medicines. At the center of all this magic, there is something small, powerful, and bright green called **chlorophyll.** *Unfortunately for the color wizard, it's hard to get this enchanted green out of tree leaves and onto paper. But there is a way. To find and use chlorophyll, you must follow a dark path, and you're going to be working with spinach, so prepare yourself...*

SUPPLY LIST

- ★ 1 cup spinach (frozen is recommended, but fresh works too)
- ★ 2 bowls (cereal size, nonstaining), plus a plate or lid to cover one of the bowls
- ★ ¼ cup isopropyl (or rubbing) alcohol (ask your assistant to help you check the medicine cabinet or local pharmacy)
- ★ Safety goggles

- ★ Spoons (wooden ones may get stained)
- ★ Strainer or large funnel
- ★ Cheesecloth, paper towels, or coffee filters
- ★ White paper (for normal painting)
- ★ Black paper (to view the fluorescence)
- ★ Washable surface, like a large baking sheet or tray
- ★ Paintbrush
- ★ Black light flashlight or light fixture with bulb

INSTRUCTIONS

1. Thaw 1 cup of frozen spinach in a microwave or on the stove top until it's steaming. For fresh spinach, chop it up roughly, then heat it. Check with your assistant before using the microwave, stove, or knife.

2. Put the hot spinach in a bowl, and carefully add ¼ cup of rubbing alcohol to it. Don't forget your safety goggles!

3. Mix the spinach a bit with a spoon, then cover the bowl with a pot lid or a plate and let it sit for 5 minutes.

4. Have a look at your liquid by pushing the spinach to the side with a spoon. It should now be a dark-green color. Stir and smush it a few times to release more color.

5. Cover the strainer or funnel with cheesecloth, a paper towel, or a coffee filter. Position it above your second bowl and pour the spinach mixture through, straining the liquid.

6. Fold the cloth or filter around your blob of spinach and squeeze out any remaining color into your bowl.

7. The green liquid you have made is your chlorophyll paint!

8. Place white and black paper on your baking sheet or tray. The alcohol may cause some of the black dye in your paper to leak through to your work area, so use a washable surface. Then dip your brush in and get painting!

9. To see the brightest green pigments of this, use white paper.

10. To see your ink glow, use the dark paper. While the paint is still wet, go into a dark room and shine a black light on your paintings to reveal the hidden plant power.

11. Your paint will last a few days in a jar with a tight-fitting lid. Just give it a stir or shake before reusing.

WHAT'S HAPPENING HERE?

Chlorophyll (the green stuff) is like a battery that soaks up the sun's energy and feeds it to the growing plant. The alcohol in this experiment separates the chlorophyll from the plant. Without any plant to feed, the chlorophyll has extra energy to give away. The energy is invisible until you shine a black light on it to see it glowing red.

TROUBLESHOOTING

If you want more paint, add a little more alcohol to the spinach and squeeze out the liquid into your bowl. If your paint is too light, let some of the alcohol evaporate by leaving the container open, but don't put it in the sun, which will turn it brown.

MORE MAGIC

- Replace the spinach with other plants. You can use your black light to find out which plants have the most hidden power in them by shining the light on their leaves. If you find a leaf outside (or in your fridge) that's soft enough to smush up and glows bright red under your light, then you have a powerful plant to test out.

- Put it in a lava lamp. Check out **The Enchanting Purple Lava Lamp** (p. 102) or use this as an activity at your **Psychedelic Sorcerer's Disco Party** (p. 148).

Copper Penny Blue Ink

TIME: 30 minutes for prep and bottling + 1–3 weeks for a full color transformation

 Copper oxide is an irritant, and the dust should not be breathed in. Brew this color in a well-ventilated area and use rubber gloves and a face mask when handling.

Copper can be found almost anywhere in a city. Pennies, copper wire, and bits of copper pipe can often be found on the street. If you, or your assistant, prefer foraging in a hardware store, copper wool or copper wire are great sources. Copper oxide can damage metal pens or other marking tools, so it's best used with a brush or dropper. Keep in mind that this is one of those recipes that can take a week or more to really develop its color. Checking in on a few mysterious jars working their magic in the corner of your lab is part of the fun.

TRUE MAGIC: It Pays to Keep Your Eyes on the Ground

If you find a penny, pick it up and check the date on it. Pennies from before 1982 are 95 percent copper. Not only do they work great for experiments, but copper has become so expensive that the metal in a penny from before 1982 is worth two cents now. And, according to penny collectors, if you happen to find a 1943 penny that is bronze instead of copper, it might be worth 1.7 million dollars.

SUPPLY LIST

- Rubber gloves
- Face mask
- Glass jar
  - ½ cup copper scraps
  - 2 cups white vinegar, plus more as needed
  - 1 tablespoon salt
  - Spoon or stirring stick
  - Coffee filter and funnel or fine-mesh strainer
  - 2 large glass containers with tight-fitting lids

INSTRUCTIONS

1. Put on your gloves and mask. In a large glass jar, cover the copper with vinegar until it's mostly submerged (leave a few pieces peeking out of the liquid). Add the salt and give your mixture a stir.

2. Leave the mixture in a well-ventilated area, uncovered, away from pets and curious toddlers, for 1–3 weeks, until you have a rich blue-colored liquid. Stir twice a day, adding more vinegar as the liquid evaporates so that the copper pieces are about half covered.

3. Once the desired hue has been reached, strain the ink through a coffee filter fit into a funnel and pour it into individual glass containers with tight-fitting lids. The color may separate into a transparent darker blue and a lighter, milkier liquid. Shaken together, these will form a beautiful drawing ink.

MORE MAGIC

⚡ This ink looks beautiful when it pools on paper, with many variations and textures. The fun here is in experimentation. The salt in this recipe acts as a catalyst for the oxidation of copper, which means that the salt helps the copper change color. It also causes the copper ink to form crystals—so try sprinkling salt on your wet paper!

⚡ Try this ink in your experiments with **Make a Martian Landscape** (p. 83).

⚡ This color also weathers nicely on a poster outdoors. See **A Color Block Party** (p. 146).

Indigo Berry Blast Blobs

TIME: 15–30 minutes

These blobs will look like they're alive. And because they are not *just* blue or purple or red, they go by the name indigo, which is the most in-between-y of colors. If you set up for a bit of a mess, then you can go really wild with this one.

SUPPLY LIST

- ★ A clean workspace protected by newspaper, plastic, or a washable covering
- ★ ¼ cup frozen blueberries, raspberries, or blackberries OR any kind of fresh, juicy, purple-colored berries that stain your fingers and aren't toxic
- ★ Glass measuring cup or beaker
- ★ 1 teaspoon baking soda
- ★ 2 tablespoons warm water
- ★ 3 small bowls

- ★ 2 tablespoons white vinegar
- ★ Fork
- ★ Fine-mesh strainer
- ★ Paper
- ★ 3 droppers
- ★ 1 wedge of lemon

INSTRUCTIONS

1. Allow the berries to begin thawing in a glass measuring cup or other pourable container.
2. Add the baking soda and warm water to the first bowl and stir.
3. Add the white vinegar to the second bowl.
4. Use a fork to smash your thawing berries until they've released their juice, then pour the juice through a fine-mesh strainer into the third bowl.
5. Put a piece of paper on your work surface and drip a full dropper of berry juice onto it from a foot or two above the paper.
6. See what happens when you use just the dropper and gravity, or get your fingers in there and do some finger painting. Once you have a design that you like, it's fun to watch the way the color changes as it dries.
7. While your artwork is drying, fill a dropper from the bowl of vinegar. Choose an area on your paper with lots of color and squirt a few drops of white vinegar onto it.
8. Try the same thing in a different area with the baking soda solution.
9. Squeeze a few drops of lemon in a different area.
10. Admire your berry-blast art.

TRUE MAGIC: Million-Dollar Drips

Jackson Pollock, who was a super-famous modern artist, got help from gravity. He made his art by dribbling paint from a bucket and letting it fall on his canvas. The drips and squiggles he made not only are beautiful but have also been studied by physicists looking to understand the science of falling and moving liquids (called fluid dynamics). What's harder to explain is why, amazing as they are, his paintings full of wild splatters have sold for more than a hundred million dollars, which, if you do the math, makes some single drips worth almost a million dollars!

MORE TRUE MAGIC: Blueberries Are Not Exactly Blue

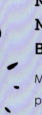

Most berries, especially dark-red, blue, or purple ones, have a pigment in them called anthocyanin. This special ingredient is what makes blueberries so good for you, and it also allows them to change color. When you add acids (like lemon or white vinegar) to the berries, they look pink. When you add bases (like baking soda, borax, or soap), they will turn blue or green. Scientists call this color-changing power pH. Your friends and family might call it magic!

COLOR HERO:
Mary Gartside, Pioneer of the Color Blob

In the early 1800s, a watercolor teacher and floral painter named Mary Gartside did something incredible. She used her observations of light and shadows among garden flowers to challenge Newton's version of the rainbow. She was the first woman (that we know of) to publish a book of color theory. As if that weren't incredible enough, the book also included a set of extraordinary abstract color tests that she called blots. Mary's inky blots, which capture the energy and spirit of color, without trying to be any one particular shape, look a lot like the experiments of the artists Wassily Kandinsky, Piet Mondrian, Kazimir Malevich, and Mark Rothko—the so-called color revolutionaries who made their discoveries over a hundred years later.

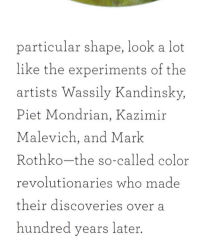

The Enchanting Purple Lava Lamp

TIME: 1 hour

Set the mood for spells, magic shows, and parties—or just give yourself some weird dreams with this natural color lava lamp.

SUPPLY LIST

- A clean workspace protected by newspaper, plastic, or a washable covering
- 2 cups chopped red cabbage
- 1 cup water
- Blender, juicer, or pot to boil water (basically, you'll need a way to get that cabbage juiced)
- Strainer
- Baking soda (you can also try borax, or even powdered dishwashing soap)
- Tall, clear glass or bottle
- 1½ cups light oil, like vegetable or canola
- Alka-Seltzer (or similar bubbling antacid tablets)

INSTRUCTIONS

1. Juice the cabbage! There are a few ways to do this. You can juice the cabbage in a juicer with water OR blend some of the darkest leaves with water and strain the juice OR boil equal parts water with chopped cabbage and strain the juice (all these methods might require help from your assistant). You can also put the leaves in salt and water overnight. Whichever way you do it, you should strain out any remaining bits of cabbage and end up with about 1½ cups of a bright-purple juice—if the color is weak, add more cabbage.

2. Put about a cup of the juice in a new container and slowly add ½ teaspoon of baking soda, mixing thoroughly until the solution is blue. (Baking soda will turn it indigo, and you can also try borax instead, which will make it teal.) If the color has not changed after adding ½ teaspoon of baking soda, dilute the juice with ¼ cup of water and add another ½ teaspoon of baking soda. The reason for doing this is that if the cabbage juice is too concentrated, one antacid tablet won't produce enough carbonic acid to change the color.

3. Fill up your tall, clear glass about ⅔ of the way with the oil.

4. Add some of the blue cabbage juice to the tall glass. It should sink to form a bottom layer; you want to add enough so you have about four times as much oil as juice. Make sure to leave room at the top of the glass because it may foam up.

5. Drop in your antacid tablet and observe!

MORE MAGIC

⚡ Go fluorescent: Try shining a black light on your purple lava lamp or try the black light with one of the following variations:

➜ Instead of cabbage juice, use the green liquid from **Green Glow-in-the-Dark Plant Energy** (p. 91).

➜ Replace cabbage juice with 1 teaspoon lemon-lime gelatin dissolved in ½ cup of tonic water.

➜ A white, globe-shaped glass light fixture (like you often find on a ceiling fan) placed carefully over your lava lamp makes it into a great crystal ball for parties.

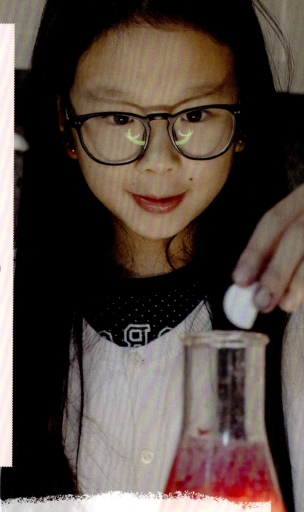

COLOR HERO:
Donna Strickland, Space-Age Rainbow Wizard

Most people would call her a physicist, but Dr. Donna Strickland, who plays with light using laser pulses, could also be called a wizard. Instead of mixing the colors of the rainbow together or splitting them up, the lasers she works with focus beams of light to move things around (kind of like the tractor beams in Star Trek). In 2018, Donna became the third woman to win the Nobel Prize in Physics because she helped invent a method called *chirped pulse amplification*, which is used in eye surgery and to shape the glass in cell phone screens. She lives in Canada (home to many color wizards), where she is part of a sort of club called the Ultrafast Laser Group.

TRUE MAGIC: The Secret Color Beyond the End of the Rainbow

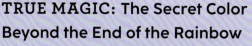

The last color in the rainbow that we humans can see is called violet, but beyond that there is a secret world of glowing purplish colors that butterflies have no problem seeing called ultraviolet (or UV) light. Flowers use UV coloring for their fanciest decorations, which don't look like much to us but are beautiful to bees and butterflies.

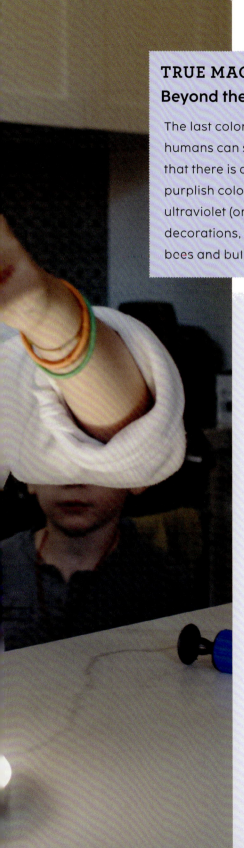

COLOR HERO: Emily Dickinson

Emily Dickinson, who made some of the best poems ever, spent most of her life alone in the garden looking at flowers and scribbling stuff down in her notebook. Her poems are so famous now that even the ones she wrote in pencil on the back of envelopes have been printed in books. Emily managed to turn being alone, noticing nature, and keeping notebooks into a very colorful life. People remember the poems but sometimes forget about her *herbarium* (a fancy name for a notebook to collect and organize plant and flower specimens). At fourteen, Emily started a collection that grew to over four hundred dried flowers. The careful noticing and reorganizing of nature found in Dickinson's herbarium can also be found in the poetry that would (eventually) make her famous.

Dark Wizard Ink

TIME: 15 minutes

(if you carbonized the sticks)

SUPPLY LIST

- ★ 10 vine charcoal sticks from the previous recipe (soft charcoal from a fire or art supply store will also work)
- ★ Mortar and pestle
- ★ 1 tablespoon gum arabic
- ★ 4–5 tablespoons water
- ★ Glass container with a tight-fitting lid
- ★ Paper

INSTRUCTIONS

1. Grind down your carbonized charcoal with a mortar and pestle until you have an extremely fine powder.

2. For every 3 tablespoons of this fine powder (or ash), mix in 1 tablespoon of gum arabic and 1 tablespoon of water into the mortar. This should give you a syrupy black liquid. Continue to stir and grind this liquid until it's silky smooth.

INSTRUCTIONS

1. Peel the bark off your twigs and cut them into crayon-size pieces.

2. Work with your assistant to build a fire in the woodstove, BBQ, or fire pit. Never make a fire alone.

3. Place sticks inside your tin or other sealable metal container and shut it tightly OR wrap them in two layers of tinfoil and squeeze it tight.

4. Have your assistant use tongs to place your tin at the center of the heat source. After about an hour, your assistant should carefully remove the tin with tongs and place it on a fireproof surface to cool. After *another hour* of cooling, your charcoal should be ready, but make sure the tin is cool before you open it. Each stick should be black and reduced in size by about a third.

5. Your vine charcoal can be stored in a clean mints container and used as a soft, erasable art material.

MORE MAGIC

- Use these black marking tools outside (they are a bit messy), where you can scrawl on rocks, sidewalks, or cave walls.
- Get a big roll of paper and do an outdoor mural where you imagine that you are in a cave and are sending a message to people (or robots) a million years from now.
- Make your charcoal into ink (see the next page).

TRUE MAGIC: Carbon, the Dark Pattern Maker

Vine charcoal is made from carbon, which is a magical ingredient. Carbon sustains life on our planet—everything that is or was alive has carbon in it. It's also an amazing pattern maker. When carbon atoms are separate, they are light enough to float, and when they're close together, they can make wood or bone or hard charcoal stick. When they're packed in tight, in a crystal shape, they make one of the hardest things in the world—a diamond.

How to Make Vine Charcoal for Ink or Drawing

TIME: 2 hours

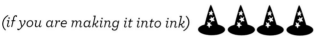
(if you are making it into ink)

 Involves fire!

Is black a color? Some say yes and some say no. Either way, if you are reading this, you are probably a Wizard of Darkness and you just want everything to be black, and I don't blame you. Let's start with a recipe for charcoal that goes back to the cave people—except you, unlike the cave people, will be using an empty box of mints.

You can buy soft vine charcoal, but it is cheaper and more satisfying to make it. Wood becomes charcoal when you heat it up without letting it catch fire. The perfect tool for this process is a mints tin—it protects the wood from burning up but has space for steam to escape.

SUPPLY LIST

- ★ 12 or so small pieces of wood or vine that fit into your container (willow twigs or grapevines work best)
- ★ Pruning shears to cut the vines or twigs to size
- ★ A woodstove, BBQ grill, or outdoor fire pit (see what your assistant recommends!)
- ★ An empty mints tin, or other tin with a lid OR 2 squares of tinfoil big enough to tightly wrap around the twigs
- ★ Tongs

2. Break up the chocolate into individual squares and put them into the 3 bags—one type in each bag. Close the bags tightly, and try to get most of the air out so the bags don't float.

3. Place the 3 chocolate-filled bags in the warm water and wait 5–10 minutes, or until the chocolate is completely melted. (You can always add warmer water from a tea kettle or microwave if the chocolate is not melting, but ask your assistant for help.)

TRUE MAGIC: Genius Squiggles

Not all doodles are the same. Personally, I like to make squiggles that follow a kind of shaky, prickly path that is called *Brownian motion*. This kind of pattern is found everywhere in nature (for example, the way bits of dust move around in a sunbeam), and Einstein even has a theory about it (see also **Million-Dollar Drips**, p. 100).

4. Lay the acetate or waxed paper or parchment on your tray or plate. Starting with the white chocolate, cut a small corner from the bag and create a wild, squiggly pattern. Use *only a third* of the white chocolate and spread out your squiggles—just be careful you don't get too close to the edge of your paper.

5. Repeat the process for another squiggly pattern using up *all* the milk chocolate and layering it on top of the white chocolate.

6. Add *all* the dark chocolate on top of your other two layers with more squiggles.

7. Carefully cover your whole design with the remaining white chocolate in a rectangular shape so that it looks like a big chocolate bar.

8. Put your tray or plate with your chocolate creation on top in the refrigerator, and chill it for an hour.

9. Remove your chocolate creation from the fridge, flip it over onto the tray or plate, remove the acetate paper, and share!

Chocolate Jackson Pollock

TIME: 90 minutes

My favorite shade of brown comes from the outside shells (or hulls) of black walnuts. These hulls are a green color at first but can be boiled to make a rich, beautiful ink. If you locate a black walnut tree in your city, you should try making it. My second-favorite brown color can be found in this popular activity that makes not only art but also a delicious treat.

SUPPLY LIST

- ★ Large bowl of warm water
- ★ ½ dark-chocolate bar (about 2 ounces)
- ★ ½ milk-chocolate bar (about 2 ounces)
- ★ ½ white-chocolate bar (about 2 ounces)
- ★ 3 clear resealable bags
- ★ 1 letter-size sheet of acetate paper (waxed paper or parchment will also work)
- ★ A tray or plate

INSTRUCTIONS

1. Fill a large bowl with warm water.

3. Add more water (about 3–4 tablespoons), a few drops at a time, until the mixture is the consistency of ink.

4. Pour it into the glass container. To further combine the water, binder, and pigment, shake the container of ink vigorously. If kept tightly capped, this ink should last forever.

TROUBLESHOOTING

Test out your ink on paper. If the color is not black enough, put the ink back in the mortar and add more carbon dust. If the ink appears grainy, you may need to grind the pigment down more, or else it needs more stirring and shaking.

TRUE MAGIC: Ancient Ink

In special containers, in secret desert caves near the shores of the Dead Sea, some of the world's oldest, most famous writing was found on scrolls. It was discovered that the writing on these Dead Sea Scrolls used the same carbon-based recipe as the Dark Wizard Ink here. And this ink is just as black now as it was when it was made over two thousand years ago!

The Secret Life of the Color Black

TIME: 10 minutes

Remember when I said I wasn't sure if black was a color? Well, here is an experiment to see what is really happening in your black magic marker.

SUPPLY LIST

- ★ Black magic marker (not permanent)
- ★ White paper coffee filter (the ones that are basket-shaped for drip machines work best)
- ★ Water
- ★ Coffee cup, mug, or plastic cup

INSTRUCTIONS

1. With the black magic marker, draw a circle on the coffee filter roughly halfway between the center and the outside edge.

2. Fold your coffee filter three times (into eighths) and open it up again. This allows you to tuck your filter into the cup without it popping out.

3. Put some water in the cup—about half an inch, or just enough to cover the bottom. Curl the edges of the paper circle up so it fits inside the cup. Make sure the bottom of the circle is in the water.

4. Watch as the water flows up the paper. When it touches the black line, you'll start to see some different colors.

5. Leave the paper in the water until the colors go all the way to the top edge. How many colors can you count?

TRUE MAGIC: Hidden Colors Can Be Useful

Not only have you discovered the hidden colors in black, you've also done something scientists call **chromatography**. Since different ingredients in a mixture are carried along by the water at different speeds, they end up in different places. By examining where all the ingredients end up, scientists can figure out what was combined to make the mixture. Chromatography is used to figure out the ingredients in different foods and perfumes and the chemicals in polluted water. Doctors even use it to find out what's in your blood (or pee!).

MORE MAGIC

⚡ Try the activity with a different kind of black marker. Does it make different colors than the first one?

⚡ Use your marker to draw a black spot in the center of a new coffee filter. Put the filter on a saucer, and add some drops of water on the spot. In a few minutes, you'll see rings of color that go out from the center of the circle to the edges.

⚡ Try other colors of markers.

⚡ Coffee filter art makes great party decorations (see p. 150).

MORE TRUE MAGIC: Black Eats the Whole Rainbow

Okay, so if black has all those colors in it, why does it look black? Well, things look dark to us when they absorb all the colors and don't bounce any light back. Things that are black have sucked up ALL the colors, so you could say black is the most color-FULL color of all.

Silvery Acorn Cap Ink

TIME: 1 hour + acorn collection time

Some people would call this color gray. But because it sparkles and is made with precious metal, the wizards have named it silver. It comes from acorns. In many places, acorns are everywhere in the fall and at the base of oak trees at any time of year. They come in all kinds of shapes and sizes, but they all have a little hat. And it's the hat that you will need for this recipe, so leave the nut part for squirrels to eat. It's fun to make this ink in a glass container because it's one of those potions that you can see changing color.

SUPPLY LIST

- 1 cup rust water (you'll find the recipe for this on p. 83)
- 1 large, old pot
- 2 cups washed acorn caps, plus more as needed
- Water
- Fine-mesh strainer
- Bowl
- Funnel
- Coffee filters
- Glass container with a tight-fitting lid
- Paper, for testing
- Gum arabic

INSTRUCTIONS

First you will need to make a cup of *rust water* (see the instructions in **Make a Martian Landscape**, p. 83).

Next, make the *acorn liquid*.

1. In a large, old pot, combine the acorn caps with 5 cups of water. Heat to boiling with your assistant, and boil uncovered for 2 hours, or until the liquid is reduced by about half. Stove-top temperatures vary, and 2 hours is a long time to boil water, so make sure you and your assistant watch the pot from a safe distance during this time.

2. Strain the resulting liquid, which should look like strong tea, first through a fine-mesh strainer into a bowl to remove large pieces. Then strain it through a funnel lined with a coffee filter into the glass container.

3. When both the rust water and the acorn liquid have brewed, pour the rust water into the container of acorn liquid and stir. Finally, test on paper.

4. The ink should be a light gray in the jar and a darker, silvery gray on paper. If it looks brown instead of silver, throw in a few more pieces of rust in the jar and wait. Once you are happy with the color on paper, you can refilter if you have added more rust. Add a dropperful of gum arabic for every 2-ounce bottle.

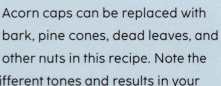

MORE MAGIC

Acorn caps can be replaced with bark, pine cones, dead leaves, and other nuts in this recipe. Note the slightly different tones and results in your Wizard's Notebook.

TRUE MAGIC: Generous Atoms Versus Greedy Atoms

You've probably seen iron. It's the hard metal in your heavy black frying pan and the older nails in your garage. Iron is in volcanoes and swords, meteorites and magnets. In the center of the earth, liquid iron creates a protective magnetic force field around our whole planet. When it comes to color making, one of the most important powers of iron is that it gets along really well with oxygen. Iron molecules are always trying to get rid of electrons, and oxygen molecules are always taking them on. In the open air, iron and oxygen make an orangey rust, and in rocks they make a beautiful red that early humans used in cave paintings. In humans, iron carries oxygen around in a lovely red liquid we call blood. So, the next time you see a rusty bolt on the sidewalk, pick it up, because it is totally magic!

Golden-Green Ink

TIME: 30 minutes for collection + 30 minutes for preparation

🧙‍♂️🧙‍♂️🧙‍♂️ 🧤

Wizards have long sought a recipe for making gold, which turns out to be a difficult process. But this is the next best thing. To make the classic sap-green recipe, you will need to find buckthorn berries, which are little black-purple berries that grow all over the world and are so yucky that even birds don't eat them. I find them in swampy areas of my local park, and usually people don't mind if you pick them because, in most places, they are considered a weed. They stain the sidewalk a purple-gray (or sometimes green) color. Buckthorn berries offer up their juiciest colors in the early fall after the first frost, when they are fully ripened and black on the branches. If you can't find buckthorn, other small, juicy, dark-colored berries like wild grapes or even frozen blueberries will work.

 As all advanced wizards know, never eat berries or plants in the wild. And especially don't eat buckthorn, a berry known to cause a particularly disgusting curse on both people and pets known as "the runs."

SUPPLY LIST

★ Large, old pot

★ 3 cups buckthorn berries (but you might want to collect several batches' worth of berries when they are at their juiciest so you have enough to really test the color)

★ Potato masher

★ Fine-mesh strainer

★ Large bowl

★ Coffee filter

★ Rubber gloves

★ 2 teaspoons borax (washing crystals)

★ ½ cup hot water

★ 2 glass jars with tight-fitting lids

★ Glass dropper

★ Paper, for testing

★ Funnel

★ Gum arabic

INSTRUCTIONS

1. In a large, old pot, crush the berries with a potato masher. Filter them through a fine-mesh strainer with a bowl underneath to collect the liquid. Discard any solids and rinse out the pot. Pour the liquid from the bowl back into the pot. A further round of filtering the liquid through a coffee filter and back into the bowl should give you a nice smooth juice.

2. While wearing rubber gloves, mix the borax in hot water in a glass jar. You will need your assistant for this. Borax isn't poisonous, but it's an irritant, so you want to be careful not to get it on your skin. Many color wizards pull out their trusty safety goggles here.

3. With a glass dropper, add one drop of the borax water at a time to the bowl filled with buckthorn juice until the color changes from purple to green. Test out the color frequently on paper.

4. Once you have the color just the way you want it, use your funnel to pour it into the other glass container or ink bottle for storage, and then add a few drops of gum arabic until you have a slightly thick, glossy ink.

TRUE MAGIC: Green Gold?

Sap green is created from an amazing and very ancient recipe from the time that ordinary people call the Dark Ages and we wizards call the Glory Days. You know those giant first letters decorated with little vines and figures (and even the occasional snail) that you sometimes see at the beginning of fairy tales? Well, all the good books, called illuminated manuscripts, started like that back in those days, which meant that monks were always running out of the most expensive colors like gold and silver for their lettering. Because sap green becomes a golden green when you get the recipe just right, it was used as a replacement for real gold.

Invisible Ink

Create secret messages, hidden codes, and sneaky maps with the dark art of invisible ink.

TIME: 20–40 minutes

SUPPLY LIST

- ★ A clean workspace protected by newspaper, plastic, or a washable covering
- ★ 1 tablespoon baking soda
- ★ ½ cup water
- ★ 2 small bowls
- ★ Cotton swabs or a paintbrush (see **Make a Wizard's Paintbrush Wand**, p. 30)
- ★ Some information that you want to share with only your most trusted wizard friends and assistants
- ★ White paper
- ★ ½ cup grape juice (or other brightly colored juice)

INSTRUCTIONS

1. Put the baking soda and water in a small bowl and mix them thoroughly.

2. Dip a cotton swab or paintbrush into the bowl of invisible ink and write your top-secret message or draw your classified drawing on paper.

3. Allow 30 minutes or so to dry.

4. To create your revealer liquid, pour grape juice into a small bowl. Dip a cotton swab or paintbrush into the grape juice and apply a thin layer of juice on the paper to reveal your hidden message.

MORE MAGIC

Now that you know how it works, you can...

- Make an invisible birthday card for someone you love.
- Give a bottle of revealer to your friend and put a seemingly blank letter in the mail to them.
- Make a treasure map that includes a few invisible details.
- Reuse your inks. Put them in fancy bottles and label them **Hide** and **Show** so you know which one is which (see **Put a Sticker on It**, p. 130).

Colors are for sharing! In this section, the color magic you've discovered will come out of its secret lair, get a name and a fancy container, and show itself off on a gallery wall, the streets of your neighborhood, or even a dance floor. Are you ready to change the colors of the world? Of course you are.

The Sorcerer's Shelf of Color Curiosities

Your wizard's shelf is the perfect place to show off your finest foraged finds and the most beautiful bottles of color you've brewed. Read on for some ideas about how to display your discoveries.

1. **Be choosy.** There is no harm in returning natural ink to nature. Your wizard's shelf should be reserved for only your finest specimens.

2. **Bottle it.** When you have a particularly magical color, find a glass bottle with a tight-fitting lid, preferably something recycled but fancy like a mustard jar, an old ink bottle, or a dropper bottle. Sterilize the glass in a dishwasher (or have your assistant put it in a pot with water and then boil it), and once it's filled, screw your lid on tight, and keep it in the fridge.

3. **Preserve it.** To preserve ink, add a clove or a few drops of wintergreen oil to your bottle. For paint, honey is a great preservative. Be aware that natural color is always changing and will fade in the sun. To preserve your work on paper, use a spray

fixative and archival paper, or take a picture of your color at its best. On the other hand, you may want to just let the color get old and mold a bit at the edges, which many wizards consider a plus!

4. **Name it.** The name you give your color is important to its magic. Knowing you, you've probably already come up with a mind-blowing name. But if you get stuck, you can always name your color something like . . .

5. **Put a sticker on it.** Most stationery stores sell stickers that can go into a printer (which is fun) or be cut down to size. But even a piece of masking tape will work. In fridges, a label keeps people from adding your art supply to a salad. On your shelf, a label reminds you where you foraged a supply, how you made it, or when you made it. It's easier to cut out the right sticker shape for your container first, then write on it, and then stick it on.

6. **Display it.** Natural color looks best on a shelf beside a cool rock, a strange piece of wood, and a dusty bottle or two. Your goal should be to claim your corner of the room while mystifying people a bit. If you don't have a shelf, display your work on paper.

A Gathering of Wizards

If you put a few wizards in a room or grassy field or city square, there is a good chance that a few magical and mysterious things will take place, and you may have a spontaneous wizard summit on your hands (though to grown-ups it may look like a regular old play date). If a wizard assistant finds themselves in the middle of a wizard summit, I recommend they let it happen—it's rarely wise to interrupt this sort of magic. If you do have time to plan, or your wizard friends seem a bit bored, I recommend one of the following group activities. Feel free to mix, match, or take these ideas in your own direction. With a little imagination, they can be adapted to any sort of weather or occasion.

THE ACORN STORE

TIME: 2 hours

*Unlike money, acorns actually **do** grow on trees, and they've been around for a lot longer. Plus, an acorn the size of a penny can grow into a giant five-hundred-year-old tree. Set up a color trading post using acorns as your currency. If your customers don't have acorns, they can pay in pennies with a date before 1982 (see **Copper Penny Blue Ink**, p. 95). This activity is sort of like a lemonade stand, except that the currency is acorns and the product is your own wizardly work!*

SUPPLY LIST

★ A place to set up that's not far from your home

★ A sign and menu (a chalkboard is good; natural chalk is great: see p. 137)

★ A small card table (or some easy-to-carry surface) and a few chairs

★ A friend or two and an assistant to help

★ Snacks and water to keep you going

★ Acorns!

★ A large jar or container for the acorns

★ Choose a few things you have made as a color wizard:

Pretty things left over from a Color Quest (p. 34)

Bottles of ink with beautiful labels (p. 130)

Natural paint sets (p. 54)

Handmade brushes (p. 30)

Handmade markers (p. 87)

Original artworks

Blank handmade notebooks (p. 21)

Homemade chalk set (p. 137)

Homemade charcoal set (p. 110)

INSTRUCTIONS

1. Choose a place in your neighborhood (or park) where there are lots of people, and make a sign to spread the word. Invite all your friends and family!

2. Set yourself up with a table and chairs, a friend and an assistant, and snacks so that you can stay awhile.

3. Put your prices on the menu. The more valuable something is, the more acorns it should cost. So, for example, a pine cone that you found at the bottom of your backpack might cost just 3 acorns, but the beautiful artwork that took you all day to make might cost 25 acorns. (You might want to keep a jar of extra acorns on hand in case some people need to borrow them to pay.)

4. Count your acorns at the end of the day and use them to make ink (see p. 118)!

MORE MAGIC

⚡ Turn your acorn stand into a trading post so that people can bring in items for you to use as color supplies and trade them for items you have made. Or you can pay them in acorn-store credits.

⚡ This same setup can also work for made-to-order mud pies in an assortment of muddy colors and decorated with natural materials.

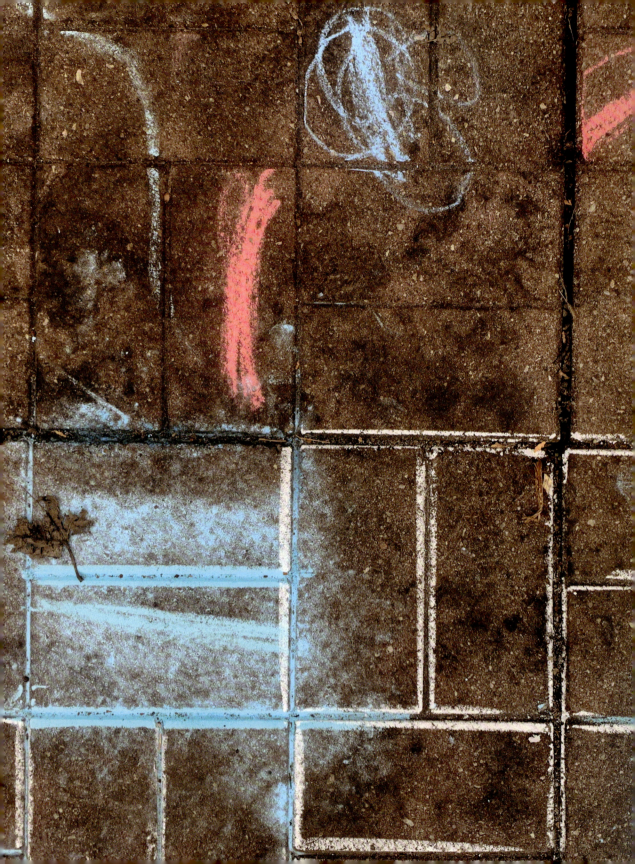

Make Your Own Sidewalk Chalk

TIME: 30 minutes + 1 day and 1 night of drying time

White, like black, is a "kind-of color." It looks like nothing when you draw with it on white paper, but put it on black paper or on a dark sidewalk and it pops! White reflects all the light back to your eyes, so it's easy to see against a dark color (which is reflecting nothing back). The white dust that goes into this sidewalk chalk gives it reflective powers—although you can add other colors to the chalk as well.

SUPPLY LIST

- ★ Plastic cups
- ★ Water
- ★ White tempera paint
- ★ Plaster of paris (dry powder, not mixed; available online or at your local arts and crafts store)

- ★ Food coloring or natural inks
- ★ Plastic spoon
- ★ Silicone mold in rectangular or square shapes (can be found in a kitchen supply store or online)

INSTRUCTIONS

1. For each color, you will need a separate cup. Begin by filling each cup with ¼ cup of water.
2. Add 2 tablespoons of the white paint and ¼ cup of plaster of paris to each cup.
3. Add 5 drops of food coloring or 10 drops of natural ink.
4. Mix well with a plastic spoon.
5. Pour the mixture into the silicone molds (the edges can be cleaned up with a paper towel).
6. If you want to layer colors, pour the first color in and add the second or third on top.
7. Let your chalk dry for 24 hours, and then remove them from the molds. Be careful because they are still soft, and you don't want to break them when you pop them out. Let them dry outside the molds for an additional 24 hours.
8. Find yourself some sidewalk and start drawing!

MORE MAGIC

- To make sparkly chalk: Try adding ground-up snail shells, mica, iridescent shellfish shells, or salt to give your chalk some sparkle.
- Magic sidewalk activities: If you have enough space, try making a giant wizard sidewalk maze (see **A Color Block Party**, p. 146) or an obstacle course.

Say It with Potatoes

TIME: 20–40 minutes

The humble potato, like the overlooked beet, is a revolutionary vegetable. It was the first food grown in space, and it is on a mission. Used on posters and flyers, it's a great way to send a message, so dig into that bag of basement spuds.

SUPPLY LIST

- ★ Sharp kitchen knife (ask your assistant to get this)
- ★ A large potato (or sweet potato)
- ★ Small cookie cutter
- ★ Paper towels
- ★ Sponges (one for each color of paint)
- ★ Natural, acrylic, or poster paints
- ★ Watercolor paper (for art), poster paper or bristol board (for posters), or a roll of paper (for wrapping paper)

MORE MAGIC

Potato printing can be used for posters, wrapping paper, cards, flags, or anything with a flat surface you want to decorate.

Instructions

The stamp

1. Have your assistant use a knife to cut a large potato in half. Position the cookie cutter in the middle of the potato half and press it down into the surface of the potato about half an inch. Then, leaving the cookie cutter in the potato, have your assistant cut away the excess potato around the cookie-cutter shape.

2. Remove any remaining bits of potato around the cookie cutter and then pull it out, leaving just the shape.

3. Dry the surface of your potato stamp with a paper towel.

The stamp pad

4. Dampen your sponges and add a squirt of paint or ink to them. (You can try a few different colors, one for each sponge stamp pad.)

5. Press your potato stamp into your sponge stamp pad to evenly cover the surface of your shape.

Printing on paper

6. Now simply press your potato stamp down on the paper you want to decorate and wait three seconds. You might want to do a test run first—after a few prints, you will know exactly how hard to press to get the look you want.

TRUE MAGIC: The Potato Goddess

Farmers in the mountains of Peru discovered how delicious potatoes were more than seven thousand years ago. While they probably never pictured people all over the world eating fries, they did understand that they had discovered something powerful. Each year a particularly odd-shaped potato would be chosen and worshipped as Axommama (or potato mother). In Incan mythology, Axommama was one of the daughters of Pachamama (the earth mother) and, if properly respected, would ensure a good harvest.

Natural Spray Paint

TIME: 5–15 minutes

SUPPLY LIST

- ★ 3 small spray bottles (available at most dollar stores)
- ★ 3 colors of natural paint, ink, or watered-down poster paint (red, yellow, and blue work great for mixing)
- ★ White paper (lots)
- ★ Tray or other washable surface
- ★ Ferns, flowers, seedpods, leaves, or other interestingly shaped plants for stenciling
- ★ Stencils (optional)

INSTRUCTIONS

1. Fill spray bottles with natural paint, ink, or watered-down poster paint.
2. Set up your paper on a tray, place a fern or other interestingly shaped plant in the middle of your sheet of paper, and lightly spray the entire page.
3. Wait a minute or two for it to dry.
4. Carefully remove your stencil plant to reveal its shape.
5. Have fun. Try other plants and flowers. And use your spray paint for good, not evil.

MORE MAGIC

⚡ Mix the colors of your spray paint by layering colors on top of each other on the paper.

⚡ What other interesting natural shapes can you try from your foraging adventures?

⚡ Use painter's tape to "mask out" your name or make other designs.

⚡ Try using stencil letters or homemade stencils.

Put the Party Together

If you've come this far, you've probably noticed that color is bouncing around, changing, and doing unexpected things. Color is not content to stay in your lab. It's alive—and ready to party!

A Color Block Party

INSTRUCTIONS

1. **Do a little planning with your assistant.** Pick a sunny-weather day and a safe spot for your block party.

2. **Get the word out.** Using potato print and/or natural spray paint techniques, make posters or flyers a few days in advance. Staple or tape them up around the neighborhood. The artwork and message are up to you, but keeping it simple lets people see it from far away.

3. **Make a neighborhood mural.** Take a close look at your neighborhood. I'm sure it's nice, but is it vibrant? It's probably time for you and your wizard companions to make the world more colorful one block at a time. Combine printing and spray paint effects on a big roll of paper or graffiti-friendly wall. Ask friends and neighbors to join in. Add stencil letters, stickers, and any leftover colors you might have for decorating.

4. **Decorate the sidewalk** (see **Make Your Own Sidewalk Chalk**, p. 137). Draw lines or arrows that people can follow to the location of your street party. Create a maze, dance floor, or other game at your chosen location.

The Psychedelic Sorcerer's Disco Party

TIME: 2 hours prep time + however many hours you can keep dancing

It might surprise you to learn that wizards love a disco party. But think about it: the mysterious darkness, the colorful lights, things that sparkle and glow, and, of course, the chance to dress up, dance, and get a little weird with other wizards. Like any good color recipe, this one requires a bit of planning, some materials, a few experiments, and a willing assistant or two, but the results are pure color magic.

SUPPLY LIST AND INSTRUCTIONS

★ **Choose a party activity:**

The Enchanting Purple Lava Lamp (p. 102)

Green Glow-in-the-Dark Plant Energy (p. 91)

Find a Rainbow in the Dark (p. 62)

Your choice of any group activity from the book

- ★ **Choose your music.** Make a playlist ahead of time—ask your friends what dance songs they like or look for songs about colors!

- ★ **Find a dance floor.** You'll need a smooth area with nothing breakable nearby. Consider having a no-shoes policy!

- ★ **Invite some friends.** Maybe you want to make fancy invitations with homemade ink! No matter how you invite people, give plenty of advance notice, and ask your guests to come wearing sparkly or colorful clothing.

- ★ **Prepare refreshments.** Have some colorful snacks and drinks on hand because dancing is hard work! Maybe you want to make a color buffet (just make sure to position it away from the dancing area!). Try offering fizzy water in clear plastic glasses, and let your friends add a drop of food coloring or edible natural ingredients to their drink.

- ★ **Some optional items for extra flair:**

    Disco ball

    Natural confetti / glitter cannon (pp. 151–152)

    Black light

    Colored lights

A Rainbow Wizard Birthday

You might like to send out invitations written in invisible ink (with instructions for revealing), decorate your backyard with hand-dyed streamers and flags, and have a paint-making station. You might want to serve a cake made from rare edible berries decorated with flowers foraged from a magic mountain. Oh! And it would be nice to have a bar that serves fizzy drinks with natural colors and flavorings. If you happen to have two or more Level 30 Wizard Assistants with a lot of time on their hands, you could do all those things with serious planning.

But let's be honest. Birthday parties are so fun that they don't really need a lot of setup. There will probably be cake. And a few of your friends. And presents. And maybe pizza. And if you ask everyone to dress up in their favorite color and meet in a park, that will make a pretty great rainbow party. The thing is, while you don't need a fancy party, you do want it to be **memorable**. And nothing says memorable rainbow party like . . .

Natural Confetti

TIME: 20 minutes (for collecting leaves and making the confetti)

Create a handful of joy for birthdays, weddings, and other celebrations.

SUPPLY LIST

- Leaves of as many colors as you can find (you can use spinach or lettuce if you are indoors)
- Sheet of paper or parchment paper
- A hole punch
- Collection bag and storage container (a paper bag or jar with a lid)

INSTRUCTIONS

1. Have all partygoers help find colorful leaves, and when you have a bagful, bring it indoors.

2. Fold a sheet of paper in half and use the hole punch to punch out bits of colorful leaves you collected onto the sheet of paper.

3. When you have a big pile, use the folded paper to tip your confetti into a jar, paper bag, or your **All-Natural Confetti Cannon** (see next page).

4. Store your confetti in a dry location.

MORE MAGIC

If you can't find colorful leaves, you can use old magazines, colored paper, dried flower petals, or mica for extra sparkle.

All-Natural Confetti Cannon

TIME: 10 minutes to make and decorate, hours of fun to play with

SUPPLY LIST

★ Paper towel and/or toilet paper rolls (you'll want enough for all partygoers)

★ X-Acto knife

★ Balloons (10–12 inches each, enough for all participants)

★ Duct tape (in a fancy color or pattern if you can find it)

★ Washi tape, stickers, or other decorating materials (optional)

★ Natural confetti (see previous page)

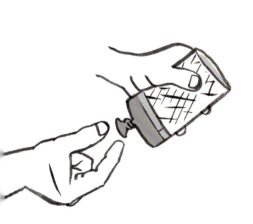

INSTRUCTIONS

1. Have your assistant cut your paper towel or toilet paper rolls into smaller tubes with an X-Acto knife. If you're using toilet paper rolls, I suggest cutting them in half, and if you're using paper towel rolls, you can cut them into quarters. You'll want your roll to be about as tall as your duct tape is wide, so you can use that as a guide.

2. Tie a knot in the bottom of your balloon, and then snip ¼ inch (6 millimeters) off the top, leaving the widest part of the balloon.

3. Stretch the top of the balloon over one cut end of your roll.

4. Cover your roll with duct tape to secure the balloon in place. The easiest way to do this is to line up the top of the cardboard roll along one edge of the duct tape and keep winding until the whole paper roll is covered. At this point, you can also spruce up your cannons with some washi tape, stickers, or other decorations around the roll if you like.

5. Fill your cannon with confetti. To use the cannon, just pull down on the knotted end of your balloon, aim, and let go!

The Last and Final Words of Advice for Wizards Who Have Made It to the End of This Book

That's it! You've collected and experimented, you've made potions and mysterious art, and you might even have a notebook stuffed full of ideas. Did you share the power of the potato with your neighbors, show your friends how to make a natural confetti explosion, or get paid in acorns? I hope you got to try all those things. If you read most of this book and tried out most of the activities, you might be a color wizard. If you have shared this magic with your family and friends and neighbors, you are very likely a color wizard. And if people have started calling you a color wizard, then I'd say you ARE one. But there is one last thing I should probably tell you about how to be a color wizard. This book is just the beginning of what you can do. Your true wizard's quest keeps going. The rest of the secrets are still out there, like a rainbow in the dark, or a mantis shrimp under the ocean, just waiting for you to discover them.

Color Wizards in Action

All of the activities and recipes in this book were tested and approved by real wizards and their assistants using foraged materials and the occasional dollar store find.

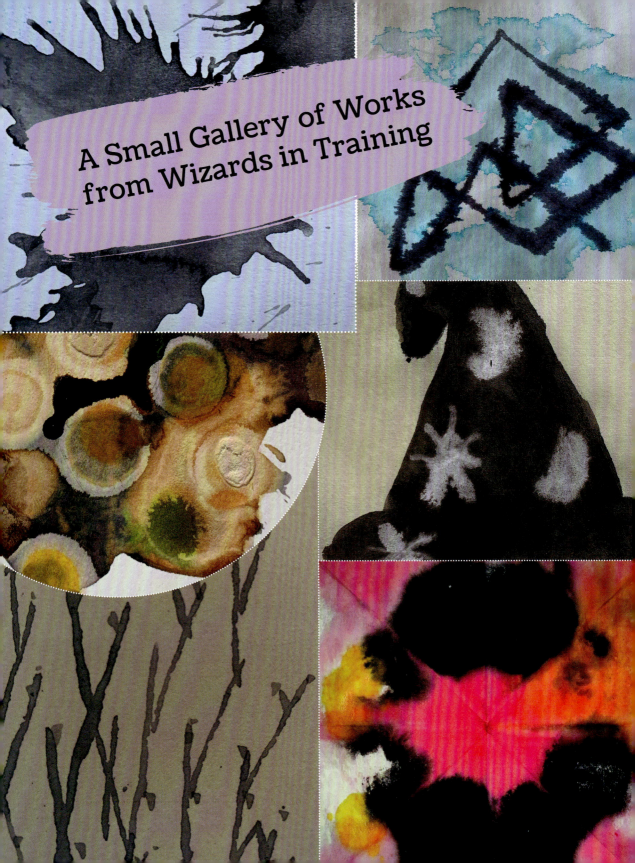

Acknowledgments

THIS BOOK WAS MADE POSSIBLE BY A WHOLE NETWORK OF WIZARDS.

My first thank-you must go to Charlotte Sheedy and Jesseca Salky, who believed in the magic when it was just a glimmer. Next to Hilary Van Dusen, who saw the glimmer and made it a spark. Maybe the biggest thank-you belongs to Olivia Swomley, my tireless editor who cast more than a few transforming spells (carefulness, optimism, and delight) over the whole project. Nancy Brennan was right beside her, an art director whose animating spells forged words, pictures, and type into a beautifully readable reality. A big thank-you goes to the essential wizards at Candlewick, including but not limited to Julia Gaviria and Emily Quill (proofreading), Emily Stone and Jason Emmanuel (copyediting), Phoebe Kosman (publicity), Rich Paradis (contracts), and Pete Matthews (editorial services). The entire team of mad scientists and magicians at Candlewick's MIT Kids Press were a joy to work with.

Thank you to the parents and assistants of the wizards and wizard testers—Antonella Castillo, Akaash Sachte, Iro Willis, Lyon Xander Clemens, Clarissa, Ruby, Winter, Arlo, Gus, Milo, Sander, Tulip, Rudy, Tomi, Sabino, Sophie, Aakash, Lyra, Evelyn, Max, Italo, Leonardo, and Mila. You are this book's secret ingredients!

In New York, my thanks go out to photographer Jason Fulford for his incredible pictures, his friendship, and his eye for finding the magic in the urban wilds of the Bronx and Queens and the Rockaways. Thank you to Jodi Levine, who came on the project as a stylist and became a talent wrangler, an inventor, a project manager, and a friend. Krysti Keener had so many roles that I will just say thank you for the alchemy and dealing with the moving van. A loud thank-you to Alva Calymayor, wizard leader of the brilliant artexperimentos and all-around fixer. Thank you to Jovana, who made the extraordinary capes! And Sarah Huck, who I thought was going to bring a few snacks and ended up making the group a glorious color feast topped off with a turmeric cake.

In Toronto, I am indebted to Chloë Ellingson (assisted by Fern) for adding photojournalism and calm beauty near the project's end and for shooting the cover in the wind under a tree on deadline. And thank you to Margot Guralnick for the inspiration and guidance. A giant thanks also to May, Alex, and Sabino, super hosts of the neighborhood color party.

Additional thanks go to Leanne Shapton, Jennifer Daniel, Olivia Bloch, Rebecca Lopez, Kelly Ruggli, Sara Vasil, William van Roden, Kristin St. Clair, Naomi Demanana, Jaspal Riyait, Irwin Adam, Lisa Naftolin, Harriet Alida Lye, Shalini Roy, Valentina Gallup, Rebecca Lopez, Markus Grupp, Judy Drydale Shapiro, Sam Henderson, Poonam Khanna-Bastin, Casey Dutfield, Sarah Azulai, Gustavo Franco, Amy Yu, Alëna Skarina, and Rūta.

This book would have been impossible without the deep knowledge of my wizard mentors, including Thomas Little (visionary wizard), Heidi Gustavson (ochre wizard), Birnur Temel (pasta wizard), Wendy MacNaughton (drawing wizard), Julia Norton (revolution wizard), Hiroaki Ooka (shadow wizard), Cara Marie Piazza (textile wizard), Ani Castillo (human wizard), Marta Abbott (Roman wizard), Yuri Shimojo (fog wizard), Karen Vaughan (soil wizard), Amy Logan (wreath wizard), Leah Logan (wise wizard), and Dwayne Gale (tape wizard). And the deep knowledge from all those mad scientists, witches, and wizards who have been part of the color network of #makeink.

Special thanks to the color residency hosts, including Julie, Jeff, Camille, Suzanne, Nick, and Carla. Extra special thanks to Winter, Soren, and Lux, who keep me real. And to Heidi, for more than words could possibly cover. And one more thank-you goes out to you reading this book right now because without readers, books cannot do any magic at all. To anyone that I am forgetting, my appreciation is bigger than my memory, so please don't put a hex on me.

In memory of Rudy (rudeboy) Shimojo.

Index

Page numbers in **bold print** indicate activities/recipes.

Acorn Store, **134–135**. See also Silvery Acorn Cap Ink
activity symbols, decoding, 11
All-Natural Confetti Cannon, 149, 151, **152–153**
Axommama, 141

beets, 49, 78–81, 88
berries, 98–99, 100, 121–123
birth trees, 32–33
black, Secret Life of the Color Black, **114–115**. See also Dark Wizard Ink
black walnuts, 42, 88, 108
blots/Gartside's inky blots, 101
blue, Copper Penny Blue Ink, 44, 85, **95–97**
Bright-Pink (Underground) Ink, **78–81**
brown, Chocolate Jackson Pollock, **108–109**. See also Pollock, Jackson
Brownian motion, 109
Bubbly, Fiery Dragon's Blood Ink, **73–76**, 85

capillary action, 68
carbon, 111
chalk, Make Your Own Sidewalk Chalk, 38, **137–139**, 146
chlorophyll, 91, 93
Chocolate Jackson Pollock, **108–109**. See also Pollock, Jackson
chromatography, 115
cinnamon, 87–89
Color Block Party, 97, 139, **146**
Color Quests: Hunt for Hidden Color
    Color Falling from the Sky Quest, **42**
    Enchanted Earth Quest, **40**
    Supernatural World Quest, **44**
    supplies and instructions, 36–37
    Wild Waters Quest, **38**
Color Wizard's Secret Guide to Making Color from Practically Anything, 37, 49, **54–57**

confetti, 42, 149, **151**, **152–153**
Copper Penny Blue Ink, 44, 85, **95–97**
curry powder, 87–89

Dark Wizard Ink, 33, 38, **112–113**
Dead Sea Scrolls, 113
Dickinson, Emily, 21, 105
dragon's runes, 76
drying time, 58

Enchanted Earth Quest, **40**
Enchanting Purple Lava Lamp, 93, **102–104**, 148
eyes, 16, 26, 27, 74

Find a Rainbow in the Dark, **62–63**, 148
flamingos, 79
food coloring, 63, 64, 138
formula for magic, 71

Gartside, Mary, 101
Golden-Green Ink, **121–123**
Green Glow-in-the-Dark Plant Energy, 42, **91–93**, 104, 148

How to Look Good: The Shrimp and the Hula-Hoop, **26–27**, 36
How to Make Vine Charcoal for Ink or Drawing, 44, **110–111**

illuminated manuscripts, 123
Indigo Berry Blast Blobs, 38, 42, **98–99**
Invisible Ink, **124–125**
iron, 83, 84, 119

kitchen, turning into a secret laboratory for mad wizardly experiments, 48–49
Kuò, Shěn, 21, 24

labeling/put a sticker on it, 88, 125, 130

magenta, Bright-Pink (Underground) Ink, **78–81**
Make a Martian Landscape, 44, **83–85**, 97, 118
Make Your Own Sidewalk Chalk, 38, **137–139**, 146
Make Your Own Wizard's Notebook, **22–25**
mantis shrimp, 26, 27

Natural Confetti, 42, 149, **151**
Natural Spray Paint, 40, 42, **142–143**
Newton, Sir Isaac, 21, 62, 70–71
note to wizard assistants, 4–5
note to young wizards, 10
notebooks, 21, **22–25**

orange, Make a Martian Landscape, 44, **83–85**, 97, 118
orange-yellow, Spicy Highlighter Markers, **87–89**
oxygen, 83, 84, 91, 119

paprika, 49, 87–89
pennies, Copper Penny Blue Ink, 44, **95–97**
Pollock, Jackson, 100. *See also* Chocolate Jackson Pollock
primary colors, 69
Psychedelic Sorcerer's Disco Party, 63, 93, **148–149**
purple, Enchanting Purple Lava Lamp, 93, **102–104**, 148

Rainbow Wizard Birthday, 68, **150–153**
rainbows
 Find a Rainbow in the Dark, **62–63**, 148
 Take the Rainbow for a Walk, **64–69**
red, 74, 84. *See also* Bubbly, Fiery Dragon's Blood Ink
red cabbage, 102–104
Roads of Blood, 38, 81. *See also* Bright-Pink (Underground) Ink
rust, 44. *See also* Make a Martian Landscape; Silvery Acorn Cap Ink

sap green, 123. *See also* Golden-Green Ink
satchels
 Assemble an Adventure-Worthy Color Wizard's Satchel, **18**
 tool up for outdoor adventure, 16

Say It with Potatoes, 57, **140–141**
Secret Life of the Color Black, **114–115**
Seven Laws of Safe Sorcery, 12–13
shells, 38, 139
Silvery Acorn Cap Ink, 40, 42, **116–119**. *See also* Acorn Store
sorcerer's shelf of color curiosities, 129–130
Spicy Highlighter Markers, **87–89**
spinach, 91, 92–93, 151
staffs, 16, 29
Strickland, Donna, 104
Supernatural World Quest, 44
supplies
 kitchen, turning into a secret laboratory for mad wizardly experiments, 48–49
 see-through sorcery/glass, 52–53
 tool up for outdoor adventure, 16

Take the Rainbow for a Walk, **64–69**
tetrachromats, 27
trees/wood, 31, 32–33, 91
turmeric, 49, 73–74, 87–89

ultraviolet, 26, 105

vine charcoal
 Dark Wizard Ink, **112–113**
 How to Make Vine Charcoal for Ink or Drawing, **110–111**
 Supernatural World Quest, 44

wands
 Make a Wizard's Paintbrush Wand, **30–33**, 38, 40, 124
 staffs and, 29
 tool up for outdoor adventure, 16
what kind of wizard are you today? (quiz), 7–9
Wild Waters Quest, **38**
wizard elements, 8–9

Jason Logan is the founder of the Toronto Ink Company (maker of ink for Margaret Atwood, Yoko Ono, Michael Ondaatje, and Harley-Davidson). His art has been exhibited in New York City, Los Angeles, Toronto, and the Yukon, and his ink-making revolution has been featured by the *New York Times*, Martha Stewart, the *New Yorker*, and NPR. His book for grown-up wizards, *Make Ink: A Forager's Guide to Natural Inkmaking*, was included in the *Guardian*'s best books of 2018. *The Colour of Ink*, an award-winning documentary film directed by Brian D. Johnson featuring his work, was a special selection at the Toronto International Film Festival in 2022. Jason Logan can be found picking up rusty nails and scavenging for berries on the streets of Toronto, where he lives with his family and a giant dog known as Baby.

Courtesy of Jason Logan